When Boston Won *the* World Series

When Boston Won the World Series

A CHRONICLE OF BOSTON'S
REMARKABLE VICTORY *in the* FIRST MODERN
WORLD SERIES OF 1903

BY BOB RYAN

RUNNING PRESS
PHILADELPHIA · LONDON

9   8   7   6   5   4   3   2
Digit on the right indicates the number of this printing

First paperback edition published in 2004

Library of Congress Cataloging-in-Publication Number 2002108934

ISBN 0-7624-1840-0

Cover photograph: Huntington Avenue Grounds
(National Baseball Hall of Fame Library, Cooperstown, NY)
Cover designed by Whitney Cookman
Interior designed by Matthew Goodman
Edited by Greg Jones
Typography: Garamond and Bank Gothic

This book may be ordered by mail from the publisher.
Please include $2.50 for postage and handling.
But try your bookstore first!

Running Press Book Publishers
125 South Twenty-second Street
Philadelphia, Pennsylvania 19103-4399

Visit us on the web!
www.runningpress.com

DEDICATION

―――――

To Conor, Jack and Amelia:
Let's hope they win one
in *your* lifetime.

ACKNOWLEDGEMENTS

Not for the first time, I am indebted to the staff of the Boston Globe Library, who must always brace themselves for a high-pitched whine, followed by some naughty words, whenever the technologically-impaired guy from the sports department discovers that the microfilm machine either won't focus properly or refuses to print.

I could not have executed this project without the great assistance provided by Jeff Idelson, Bill Francis and Jim Gates at the Baseball Hall of Fame in Cooperstown, N.Y. The A. Bartlett Giamatti Research Center is a marvelous resource, and its services are open to anyone, not solely professionals. W.C. Burdick of the Baseball Hall of Fame Library and Jack Grinold of Northeastern University were invaluable in providing photographs.

Carlo DeVito and Greg Jones of Running Press get my thanks for involving me in this project. There are very few occasions when any author can truthfully say that he or she actually enjoyed writing a book, but this was one of those delightful exceptions.

And to you, Tim Murnane, I wish I could have been sitting next to you when Big Bill Dinneen fanned Honus Wagner to end the final game of the 1903 World Series, and thus "proclaimed the downfall of the mighty man and his nine."

CONTENTS

HUNTINGTON AVENUE GROUNDS, BOSTON

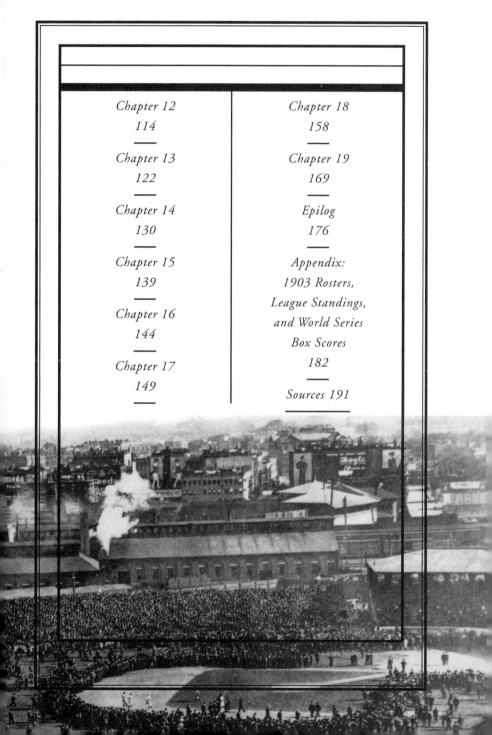

INTRODUCTION

The bases were 90 feet apart. The pitcher's mound was 60 feet, 6 inches from home plate. Three strikes meant you were out and four balls meant you could take your base. There were three outs per inning and a game consisted of nine innings. The bat looked like a bat and the fielders wore gloves.

Of course, those gloves barely covered a player's hand. Catchers' equipment was likewise primitive by our standards. And when management was faced with an overflow crowd the custom was to allow people onto the outfield surface and place a rope up to separate them from the outfielders. Ground rules were then established to cover the contingency of a baseball being hit into the crowd.

Rosters were small. There was no such thing as a "relief pitcher."

The team who would emerge as the winner of the first World Series employed five pitchers for the entire season.

There were no dugouts. Players sat on benches and had interaction with the customers. There were no public address systems. Announcements were made via megaphone. Uniform numbers were a couple of decades away.

But the basic game of baseball has hardly changed in the ensuing one hundred years. The dynamics of the game remain the same, as you will see. People loved the game for the same reasons they love it now, and in 1903 no city loved its baseball more than Boston, Massachusetts. It was entirely appropriate that the city of Boston be gifted with a team good enough to win the first World Championship of the twentieth century.

Much of what you will read has been filtered through the eyes of a remarkable man named Timothy Murnane. Tim Murnane had been a player himself, but now he was day-to-day chronicler of American League baseball for the *Boston Globe*. Reading his accounts, I felt an incredible kinship and bonding reaching down through the ages. I envied him for knowing Cy Young, and for being able to see him pitch. I envied him for knowing the gracious Jimmy Collins, a gentleman scholar-athlete who set the defensive standard for all third basemen to come, and who was an inspirational leader. And I am sure he would have been equally thrilled to see the likes of Pedro Martinez and Nomar Garciaparra.

The Boston Red Sox routinely draw two and a half million people to their ballpark nowadays. Their games are followed religiously on television, radio and through the newspapers. They are enormously big business. But, as appreciated as they are, they are not one bit more popular or important to the lives of the local citizens, than they were a century ago.

You think baseball matters in Boston now? Come back with me to 1903. You will find a passion for baseball, and for the local American League baseball team, that has never been surpassed.

GLOVES IN 1903—AS WITNESSED HERE ON HONUS
WAGNER—BARELY COVERED PLAYERS' HANDS.

CHAPTER 1

TIM MURNANE KNEW SOMETHING ABOUT
BASEBALL, AND BALLPLAYERS. HE HAD PLAYED BOTH
INFIELD AND OUTFIELD FOR PROFESSIONAL BASEBALL
TEAMS BACK IN THE 1870S AND 1880S AND HAD
BEEN A MEMBER OF BOSTON'S ENTRY WHEN THE
NATIONAL LEAGUE BEGAN PLAY IN 1876.

Now, in March of 1903, Tim Murnane was perhaps the most respected name in baseball writing. His *Boston Globe* musings stamped him as the Peter Gammons of his day. When Tim spoke on matters baseball, it was pretty much *ex cathedra*.

And speaking of prescience, how about a man stumping for the DH exactly 100 years ago? "The idea of giving the pitcher the option of sending up a substitute batter is well worth consideration," said Tim Murnane in February of 1903, "as the sight of a tired pitcher strolling to the plate to go through his usual strike out act is not an attractive feature of the game." As a further alternative, Mr. Murnane suggested that batting orders only include eight men, leaving the pitcher's spot out entirely.

The two professional baseball teams in Boston were preparing for spring training, and Tim Murnane would be following the American League club, then entering its third year of play and known, alternately, as the "Puritans," "Pilgrims," the "Plymouth Rocks," or even the "Somersets" (after Charles Somers, the original owner). They wouldn't become known as the "Red Sox" until the 1907 season.

The team had chosen Macon, Georgia as its training site, and this seemed to meet with everyone's approval. "Boston will go to Macon," Murnane had reported on March 8, "where it can practice with the college boys on good grounds, have good hotel accommodations and a warm but dry climate."

But what would happen once they arrived? That's what Murnane wanted to know, and a few days later he unburdened himself. "The place to train players is on the ball field," Murnane declared. "A player will chase a ball all day on the field who would be disgusted with a run on a country road. I believe the players should be taken from the hotel to the grounds, allowed to practice all they please and then return for a fine bath and rubdown.

"The players should not be asked to walk to the hotel from the ball grounds after a hard practice," he continued. "Sometimes they have to go two or three miles, often with spiked shoes, and when they are dead tired. I have seen a manager make the players walk nearly three miles to the grounds for morning practice. The chances are the boys are not any too anxious for work after such a walk and lacked the snap they would have shown had they been feeling fresh."

Obviously, Marvin Miller and Donald Fehr were far in the future.

Welcome to the 1903 world of major league baseball. The game was indeed America's "national pastime," and it was populated with players who were being asked to play with "snap" and "ginger." It was a rough game whose system of justice was equal parts Old Testament, King Arthur's Court and Dodge City. Some viewed it as an unsavory profession. Many a mother would have heartily disapproved had her daughter brought home a baseball player and introduced him as her beau. Illiterates almost undoubtedly out-numbered college men.

But people loved the game, even if they didn't always respect the men who played it for money. By 1903 baseball had been a vital part of American life for half a century, long enough for there to be "good, old days where men were men" and not the "crybabies" of today.

The game of a century ago was certainly recognizable as baseball, but it was still at best a first cousin to the game we know today. The baseball was not very lively, and there were as many inside-the-park home runs as balls that actually went over the fence. The typical glove barely covered a player's hand and was either left on the field or stuffed into his back pocket when his team was at bat. Rosters were small. Pitchers were expected to complete what they started. There were two umpires, and quite often it was very difficult to maintain control of the game.

Turning people away who wanted to come inside was a very difficult concept for owners to grasp; hence the universal practice of allowing people to spill onto the outfield with ropes put up in front to

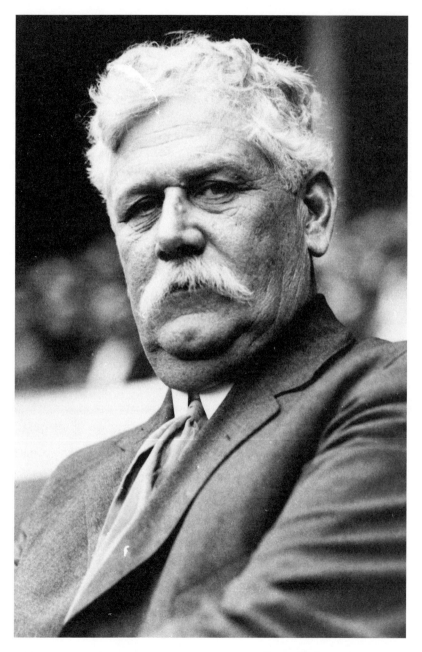

TIM MURNANE, BASEBALL EDITOR OF THE *Boston Globe* FOR THIRTY
YEARS, WAS ALSO A NOTABLE PLAYER, MANAGER, LEAGUE OFFICIAL,
AND AN IMPORTANT FIGURE IN THE GAME'S EARLY YEARS.

accommodate ground rule doubles or triples.

Rules were still evolving. The National League had adopted the so-called foul-strike rule we know today in 1901, with any foul ball being a strike. But the American League was just adopting the rule for the 1903 season, and not everyone was pleased. A *Boston Herald* poll revealed that a staggering 95 percent of its respondents were against the foul strike rule. There was, of course, no radio or television, and so there were no unwelcome commercial interruptions. A game lasting two and half-hours was considered inordinately pokey.

All games were, of course, played in daylight, with the traditional weekday starting time being 3 p.m.

The players were smaller. Anyone over 6-feet or weighing more than 190 pounds was certifiably big.

But the game was basically the same. Check out any ballpark picture dating as far back as the 1870s, and what you see is a very recognizable baseball field. By 1903 there were three strikes, four balls and three outs and there was the same inherent timeless drama that characterizes this great game. The game was still rough, but nowhere near as savage as it had been in the 1890s, when cheating and intimidation was the norm and many decent people were scared away from the game. The people who ran baseball knew the game had to change and broaden its demographic appeal (i.e. stop offending women), and so it did.

A century ago, baseball was unchallenged as American's most popular sporting activity, and Boston has as good a claim as being the epicenter of baseball interest as any city in the land. A Boston team calling itself the Red Stockings had dominated a league called the National Association from 1872-75, winning four consecutive pennants. The '75 squad had a startling 71-8 record that included a 37-0 record at the original South End Grounds, Boston's primary baseball facility from 1871-87.

The team entered the National League in 1876, and today calls itself the Atlanta Braves. That's continuity.

Its Golden Era was the Gay '90s, when the club battled the Baltimore Orioles for the right to call itself the "Team of the Decade." Boston won National League pennants in 1891, 1892, 1893, 1897 and 1898. In addition, a Boston team won the only Players League pennant race available in 1890, and yet another Boston team won the rival American Association title in 1891.

With five pennants to savor, and that long history as a solid franchise, the Boston Nationals—"Bean-eaters" to some—had to feel they were in a solid position when the American League launched its challenge in 1901. But with star players such as third baseman Jimmy Collins, pitcher Big Bill Dinneen, and outfielder Chick Stahl jumping from the Nationals to the Americans, the fans, or "cranks," as they were universally known in those times, demonstrated that their loyalty was to the players who were actually wearing the uniforms and not the flannels themselves.

The irrefutable fact is that Boston became an American League city as soon as the first game was played in 1901. It didn't hurt that the Americans impressed the fans by charging a quarter for entry, as opposed to the Nationals' fee of fifty cents, but there was more to it than simple economics. Almost from the moment of their inception, the Americans became the "In" team in town.

Attendance figures don't lie. The new American League team came frighteningly close to doubling its rival's attendance (289,448 to 148,502) in 1901, the first year of official American-National competition. It was even worse in Year 2, when the Americans came close to *tripling* the Nationals' attendance (348,567 to 116,960), a disparity even more disheartening to the older club since both teams finished third in their respective leagues.

In the 51 seasons of two-team major league baseball before the Braves headed for Milwaukee shortly before the start of the 1953 season, the National Leaguers out-drew the American Leaguers a scant seven times, all between 1921 and 1933, when the Red Sox, stripped of all their star players by a succession of trades with the Yankees, finished eighth (last) nine times and seventh twice.

A good case can be made that the public infatuation with the new American League team had more to do with the presence of Jimmy Collins in a Pilgrims' uniform than anything else. For the elegant third baseman was far more than merely a talented athlete. He was a man of true stature.

Born in Buffalo on January 16, 1870, the son of a policeman broke into the big leagues in 1895 and by his third year was being acclaimed as a nonpareil third baseman. The story goes that his manager in Louisville (then a National League club), tiring of the way the Baltimore Orioles were bunting successfully on incumbent third baseman Walter Preston, brought Collins in from the outfield one day. And that was the end of bunting against Louisville.

Here is Baltimore manager Hughie Jennings' version: "We didn't bunt that day since he was taking over on third as an emergency, and as a favor. After that, we didn't bunt toward third base as a favor to ourselves. Good old Jimmy, who was afraid of bunts, became the death of bunts in a few weeks time. No third baseman ever matched him in fielding bunts."

It wasn't just bunts. Collins dramatically expanded the range of a third baseman, making plays to his left, to his right, in front of him and even behind him that had never been seen before. Wrote Jacob B. Morse, editor of the indispensable *Sporting Life,* "He is different from all other players in his position. His quickness of eye, his judgment, his strength of arm, his accuracy and his dexterity are something phenomenal.

"The most difficult balls find their way into his hands as if by magic. Whether the bound was long or short, high or low, on one side or the other, or if it comes up on the most difficult pick-up imaginable, it can not escape him, and is never too quick to elude him. His plays back of the bag are wonderful, and his throws are so strong that he can catch the fastest runner."

He wasn't a bad hitter, either, leading the National League in homers with 15 in 1898.

Morse further observed that "Collins proves a ball player is born, not made," because "no amount of drilling can produce such a finished production as this."

And there was more. "He has made the most of a skilled education received in his home in Buffalo," Morse gushed. "He is a skilled conversationalist and there are very few people outside of baseball who can write in as fine a hand."

Wow. Great defensive plays, base hits, and superb penmanship, too. What more could anyone ask?

JIMMY COLLINS

He carried himself with such dignity that when Ban Johnson and Clark Griffith began to enact a battle plan to combat the National League they decided it was essential to snatch Collins away from the National League and put him in Boston's American League uniform, promising him that he could not only play third base for the team, but manage it, too.

He made the move for a signing bonus of $3,100, a salary of $10,000 and the promise of 10 percent of the profits over $25,000.

Under Collins' guidance, the team finished second in 1901 and third in 1902. Connie Mack's Philadelphia Athletics were the defending champion, and while few were picking the Boston team to upend the A's in 1903, in part because there were no prospective daily lineup changes, save, perhaps, behind the plate (where veteran Lou Criger was thought to be wearing out), at least one sage thought the Pilgrims might pose a bit more of a challenge.

"Their pitching is as good as any," proclaimed Charles Comiskey, famed owner of the Chicago White Sox.

The primary pitchers were Cy Young, now 36 and a veteran of 13 seasons who was coming off a routine 32-11 season; Bill Dinneen, a right-hander who had gone 21-21 in '02; George Winter, a tiny right-hander who had compiled a 27-21 record during his first two seasons in Boston; rookie right-hander Norwood Gibson; and Long Tom Hughes, a somewhat eccentric right-hander who had been picked up from Baltimore late in the previous season.

Comiskey's prophecy turned out to be accurate. Those five pitchers would divvy up each and every one of the team's 91 wins, with earned run averages ranging from 2.08 (Young) to 3.19 (Gibson).

As camp unfolded, there was but one issue, and that was the catching job. Daily dispatch after daily dispatch discussed catching. Lou Criger was the best man and, more importantly, he was Cy Young's man. They had become a battery seven years earlier in Cleveland, had gone to St. Louis together in 1899, and had come to Boston together in 1901. But Criger, never robust, was in poor health during training camp and could not be relied upon to be the starter. It would not be hyperbolic to label catching a Boston crisis.

So it was that *Charley Farrell* was greeted as a visiting dignitary when he arrived a few weeks into training camp.

To paraphrase a famous late-twentieth century American commercial, nobody didn't like Charley Farrell, a.k.a. the "Duke of Marlboro." That would be Marlboro, as in Marlboro, Massachusetts. Farrell was born in Oakdale, Massachusetts on August 31, 1866, but he was pretty much embraced by all of Central Massachusetts, as indeed he was by all of baseball. A man of unfailing good humor, Farrell was also a pretty decent major league catcher who had toiled for eight teams in three major leagues. Most of all, he was considered to be A Good Man To Have Around.

Bob Wood was doing the catching when Farrell arrived, but Tim Murnane assured his readers that particular silliness would soon end. "Capt. Collins will pay no more attention to catcher Bob Wood, as Farrell is in every way a better man for the team," Murnane declared.

The veteran scribe sounded even happier than the "captain"— Collins was never referred to as the "manager" by the Boston press—to have Farrell aboard. "Farrell is one of the best-natured ball players alive, and is already a warm favorite with the players here," said Murnane, soon after Farrell's arrival.

"It has been the ambition of my life to play near my home in Boston," Farrell said, "and I am sure I will like Jimmy Collins and the members of the American team."

There was just one problem. Farrell was 36 and had missed neither a meal nor a pint in many a year. As far back as 1891 one scribe had declared him to be a "champion clam eater," while another one had suggested that "next to baseball, eating is his favorite pastime." A charitable Murnane was compelled to note that "The Duke says he will work off 30 pounds before the opening of the season, and will be strictly in it."

The team completed its training in Macon and then turned north on the traditional barnstorming tour. It was the same basic lineup that had finished third in 1902.

The first baseman was George (Candy) LaChance, a native of Waterbury, CT, who had started his baseball career as a catcher before being converted to first base by Charles Ebbets, of later Dodger fame. He could flash some serious leather, prompting an obituary writer to observe that "though anything but a showy player, LaChance was a wonder in fielding bad throws and in handling balls when long reach was required and was exceptionally accurate in handling fly balls. His hitting was hard and timely."

At second was another New Englander, one Albert (Hobe) Ferris, a good-field, no-hit type. Three years later he would become the infamous Hobe Ferris by virtue of a brutal fight with teammate Jack Hayden in which the little second baseman kicked the outfielder in the face. We'll just call him "fiery" and move on, except to note that no less an expert than Charles Comiskey once said that "I never saw anything better than the (second base) playing of Ferris in his early days." Comiskey added that "it was his weakness with the bat that was his undoing."

The shortstop was Freddy Parent, a runty sort (5-5, 158) who was both as quick and as big a crowd favorite as you'd think he'd be. Freddy, the pride of Sanford, Maine, would achieve notoriety simply by hanging around. He lived long enough to expound to any and all on the 1967 Red Sox, dying in 1972 just 23 days shy of his 97th birthday. To his grave he was able to proclaim, with plenty of supporting anecdotal evidence, that he had outplayed the legendary Honus Wagner in the 1903 World Series.

Collins was the third baseman, and no more need be said.

In left was Pat, or Patsy, Dougherty, who had broken into the big leagues very nicely in 1902 by hitting .342. He was looking so good in spring training that his skipper boldly predicted that he would make a run at the batting title. The center fielder was Chick Stahl, a quality hitter who had twice hit over .350 and was, at age 30, pretty much at the apex of his game. In right field was John (Buck) Freeman, another Boston Nationals expatriate who was one of the reigning dead-ball era sluggers. Freeman had knocked out 25 homers in 1899, and that would remain the standard until Babe Ruth smashed 29 in 1919.

Catching was the trouble spot, although Farrell's presence, however Falstaffian, made everyone feel better. And in case Captain Collins forgot, Tim Murnane was there to remind him.

"After his severe sickness last season, Farrell was troubled with weak legs, but long walks last winter, hand ball and bathing has put the old favorite in grand condition for this season," Murnane reported. "He should make Collins a rattling good man, as he is a brainy player and one who will keep the boys good-natured at all times."

Captain Collins was pleased enough to border on cockiness.

"I see no reason to apprehend a bad showing by the Boston team," he declared as his team prepared to break camp and head north. "On the other hand, I am sure the team will be heard from when the game is well on. There is not a man on the team who is not in fine condition (apparently, the Duke didn't count), and by the time they reach home they will be ready for the work I have cut out for them. I realize the fact that we are in fast company, but it is fast company we like because we consider ourselves about as fast as any of the teams against which we will be pitted.

"My outfield is as fast as any I know in the American League, while in the box I have all the confidence any manager should have. Behind the bat, none of the teams can beat me. I am satisfied."

And so was Tim Murnane.

The great scribe was ecstatic about the five-man pitching staff. "Cy Young is burning them in as fast as ever...Billy Dinneen is in better shape than for many seasons...George Winters, who was down to 80 pounds last summer during his sickness, now weighs nearly double that...Gibson is a medium-sized, well-built fellow with fine control and a cool head...Tom Hughes looks good. Boston took him from Baltimore last season when his arm was gone, and nursed him to the finish for the sake of having him on the list this season. If he comes around all right—and everything points that way—Collins will have a marvelous string of pitchers."

Finally, there was Captain Collins, as opposed to third baseman Collins. Murnane was full of admiration.

"Jimmie Collins had very little to say to a player, on the field or off," Murnane reported. "Working with the men gave him a different hold on his subjects. When they made an error, Collins actually turned away. He seldom commented, but allowed the player to think it over and mend his ways. Collins simply set the example. He smiled all through his work and gave the impression that he was indifferent. Such was not the case, however. He watched every move, and now and then, when walking off and on the field, he would make some quick suggestion that was sure to be well considered, and about which there was no chance for an argument. Off the field Collins often made a joking remark for the benefit of the boys, but there was never an instance where it looked like a case of call down."

The 1903 Boston Americans were ready to play some serious baseball.

TOP ROW: CHARLES FARRELL, LOUIS CRIGER,
THOMAS HUGHES, JACOB STAHL
SECOND ROW: DENTON "CY" YOUNG, WILLIAM DINEEN,
GEORGE WINTERS, NORWOOD GIBSON
THIRD ROW: GEORGE LACHANCE, JAMES COLLINS, HOBE FERRIS
BOTTOM ROW: FRED PARENT, PATRICK DOUGHERTY, JOHN O'BRIEN,
JOHN FREEMAN, CHARLES STAHL

CHAPTER 2

FENWAY PARK WAS IN THE FUTURE. THE 1903 BOSTON
AMERICANS WOULD BE PLAYING THEIR HOME GAMES AT THE
HUNTINGTON AVENUE GROUNDS, A FAR LESS IMPOSING
BALLPARK, BUT ONE WHICH WAS VERY MUCH IN KEEPING
WITH THE TIMES.

Steel and concrete parks were unknown. Ballparks were made out of wood, and were, naturally, very susceptible to fire. In fact, the park occupied by the Boston Nationals had been built to replace the celebrated South End Grounds #2, a lovely edifice that featured stately spires and which was the only legitimate double-decked park ever built to play baseball in in the city of Boston until it was destroyed by fire in 1894.

According to Michael Benson, author of *Ballparks of North America*, South End Grounds #2 "had the most distinctive grandstand of its time, a steep, majestic beauty, though certainly not the most comfortable for the spectators. . . . The Grand Pavilion was a double-decked grandstand, highest of its day, rivaled only by the bunting-covered structure on the Old Polo Grounds."

Its shelf life was brief. Constructed in 1888 to replace a park that had served Boston professional baseball interests since 1871, South End Grounds #2 caught fire in the right field bleachers and burned to the ground on May 15, 1894, a year, according to Mr. Benson, "so many ballparks burned that there were rumors of a conspiracy."

After spending a little more than a month at the cozy Congress Street Park (built to accommodate the Players League franchise of 1890), the Nationals replaced it with South End Grounds #3. Because the opulent South End #2 had been underinsured, the Nationals had to settle for a more modest single-decked structure.

The Americans needed their own place to play in 1901, and, with the help of Philadelphia owner Connie Mack, who leased the land for them (getting the American League off the ground was very much a we're-all-in-this-together venture), the Americans built a park on a site that had long been used for circuses and carnivals.

What they got for their money would be thoroughly unimaginable today. The soil was so abused that there were fairly large sandy patches of ground in the outfield where grass never did grow. A toolshed located in deep center was in play. Of course, this was not really much of a logistical problem since the distance to the far reaches of the park was 530 feet when the park opened in 1901. By 1908 it was 635 feet. The left field distance remained constant for the 11-year life of the park at 350. Right field started out at 280 and eventually settled in at 320 in

1908, remaining at that distance thereafter.

What made the Boston baseball stadium situation so interesting was that the parks sat practically side-by-side. Much has been made over the years concerning the startling proximity in New York City of the Polo Grounds, constructed in 1911 (the fifth structure bearing that name), and Yankee Stadium, constructed in 1923. They were separated by the Harlem River.

But the South End Grounds housing the Boston Nationals/Bean-eaters and the Huntington Avenue Grounds housing the Boston Americans/Pilgrims were separated by a set of railroad tracks. Never in American professional sport has there been such overtly direct competition.

BILLBOARDS CAN BE SEEN (TOP LEFT) INSIDE SOUTH END GROUNDS,
WHICH STOOD JUST ACROSS THE RAILROAD TRACKS FROM
HUNTINGTON AVENUE GROUNDS (FOREGROUND).

The Nationals had been such a success over the years—remember those five pennant-winning years in the Nineties—that in the beginning American League president Ban Johnson had been wary of entering Boston. But famed Boston sportswriter Bill Cunningham reported in a 1955 essay that Johnson had once explained to him that he decided to roll up his sleeves and fight because of "the refusal of the National League executives even to talk to him," convincing him that "he would fight them to the death in their own territories."

Opening Day 1901 demonstrated to Johnson that the Boston incursion was a sound idea. In head-to-head competition the established Nationals, playing host to the defending champion Brooklyn Superbas, drew 2,000 people, each of whom could hear the cheering of the 11,500 crammed into the Huntington Avenue Grounds to see the new Americans, featuring prize pitching acquisition Cy Young, defeat Connie Mack's Philadelphia A's, 12-4. That statement pretty much set the Boston baseball tone for the next half-century, or until the Braves gave it up after drawing a paltry 281,278 in 1952 and moved the team to Milwaukee.

So it should not have come as a surprise two years later when, on April 20, 1903, the clubs again went head-to-head on the occasion of the American League team's Opening Day (the National Leaguers had begun play a few days earlier) and the American League team scored a bloody TKO in the Battle of the Box Office.

In yet another reminder how much times have changed, each team played a doubleheader. But as a reminder that the more things change the more they so often stay the same, they were separate-admission morning-afternoon affairs. Each team split, the Nationals beating

Philadelphia in the morning and losing in the afternoon, and the Americans losing to Mack's Philadelphia club in the afternoon after beating them in the morning.

But the big story was in the head-counting department. The combined attendance for the two Bean-eater games was 5,694. The combined attendance for the two Pilgrims' games was 27,568, including a staggering 19,282 at the afternoon contest.

This was, of course, a new Boston baseball record. Tim Murnane was dazzled. "Before the game was started," he reported, "the grounds were completely surrounded by a wad of humanity, many women in the crowd unable to get into the pavilion. The crowd was held well back against the bank in left field and close to the fence, and yet ground rules were made, allowing three bases when the ball was hit into the crowd." Pat Dougherty, Chick Stahl, Buck Freeman and Freddy Parent were beneficiaries of the three-base largesse for Boston; Topsy Hartsel, Lave Cross, Socks Seybold and Ollie Pickering took advantage of the situation for Philadelphia.

There was nothing odd about all this. Allowing fans to stand in the outfield was a far more preferable course of action for any contemporary owner to enact than sending frustrated fans home with unspent cash in their pockets. This practice would last well into the new century.

"The new (business) manager, Joseph Smart, deserves praise for the able manner in which he took care of the crowds," reported the redoubtable Tim Murnane. "There were plenty of policemen present and all knew their business, although one of the bluecoats received a bad roast for taking a schoolboy from deep center past the crowd to the entrance."

AMERICAN LEAGUE PRESIDENT BAN JOHNSON

But at least one observer thought the Boston management had underplayed the affair. Writing in the prestigious weekly *Sporting Life,* Jacob Morse declared that in the ceremonial aspect of Opening Day, the Boston Americans had been "cold as an iceberg," adding that "nothing was done to signal the beginning of the season except to take the money; no invitations, no music, no prominent party to throw out the first ball."

Predictably, Murnane chose to spend a great deal of his writing space on one individual. "The feature of the day was the reception to Charley Farrell, the Duke of Marlboro, and his all-round, grand ball playing," Murnane gushed. The great scribe related how his (apparent) favorite player "threw out five men that attempted to steal second, showing that his salary wing was in apple-pie order, and got in three timely hits out of six times at bat, besides a perfect sacrifice," and how "he made light work of it behind the bat and was cheered several times for his playing."

Murnane was only reflecting the sentiments of the fandom, for an amazing thing took place when Farrell came to the plate for the first time in the afternoon game. A presentation of a diamond ring was made to him on behalf of the "Royal Rooters," the famed Boston fan brigade led by celebrated saloon keeper Michael "Nuf Ced" McGreevey (so named because when he decided an argument had run its course he would invariably halt it by bellowing, "Nuf Ced!"). This, explained Murnane, was because the Rooters "were delighted to see Farrell back to the city where he helped win a championship in '91 at the Congress Street Grounds."

The Boston batting order submitted by Captain Jimmy Collins on

Opening Day was the same for both games, excluding pitchers:

Players	Position
DOUGHERTY	*LF*
COLLINS	*3B*
STAHL	*CF*
FREEMAN	*RF*
PARENT	*SS*
LACHANCE	*1B*
FERRIS	*2B*
FARRELL	*C*

With one exception, this would be the same batting order for every game of the 1903 World Series, a confrontation no one knew would be taking place when the season began. It was the sort of continuity a modern manager could only fantasize about.

CHAPTER 3

THE 1903 BOSTON AMERICANS DID NOT GET OFF TO A
ROARING START. THE TEAM DROPPED THREE OF ITS FIRST
FOUR GAMES, AND EVEN A WINNING PERFORMANCE BY CY
YOUNG IN GAME 5 WAS NOT ENOUGH TO WIPE AWAY THE
EARLY GLOOM BECAUSE THAT SCORE HAD BEEN 2-1 AND
THE BOSTON BATS REMAINED DISTURBINGLY QUIET.

"The batters," wrote Murnane, "are not hitting up to their gait, and, therefore, not confident of batting out victories."

There was one exception. Lovable old Charley Farrell was swinging a mighty stick down in the eighth spot in the order, banging out 9 hits in his first 16 trips for a robust .563 average. But on April 27 everything changed. In a game at Washington, Farrell was on first base via a single when the thought flashed into his head that stealing second would be a good idea. He caught his spikes in the bag as he slid in and broke his right leg, just above the ankle. The estimable Duke of Marlboro would be out five months.

Like it or not, the new number one catcher would have to be Lou Criger.

It's not as if Criger was a bad player. Quite the contrary. Lou Criger was an acclaimed defensive catcher, and he was a particular favorite of Cy Young, his batterymate in both Cleveland and St. Louis. But something always seemed to be wrong with him. Farrell had been acquired precisely because Criger was seldom available to play during the early part of spring training.

What people did not know was that Criger was even then suffering from the early ravages of the tuberculosis that would one day require the amputation of a leg and would eventually kill him. He would miss almost the entire 1906 season (7 games) and he very nearly died in 1915, when he was 43 years old. But he lived until 1934, spending the last 10 years of his life in Tucson, where he had settled in the hopes of maintaining some semblance of good health.

Cy Young thought he was aces; that's for sure. "The pitcher and catcher must work together as a team," Young once explained in a 1908 interview. "Each must have the fullest confidence in the other and be able to rely upon each other at every juncture. Criger has never failed me. As a backstop, as a thrower, for quick intelligent action he ranks with the best who have ever handled a ball. Although he had the misfortune to meet with a serious illness two seasons ago that threatened to end his baseball days, he fought it and by pure grit and determination got back into the game, and there are few who can handle a bat with him and there is no man more dreaded by base runners.

"It means a lot to a pitcher to know that the man behind the gun will nab your ball, provided that he can get one hand on it, and many a time I have known him to arrest the progress of a widely pitched ball I believed he would be unable to reach at all. I have seen him again and again get in the way of balls most catchers could not have blocked and not only that, but succeeded in heading off base-runners after such plays. Passed balls and wild throws are extremely rare with him. Few men keep men closer to their bases than he, and few catchers have caught more men napping than he."

This, from the man after whom pitching's greatest award is named.

Cy Young was Criger's greatest and most impassioned admirer, but hardly his only one.

On September 8, 1930 the *Boston Post* sponsored an old-timers day at Braves Field. It was a grand and festive day, and a great many big names turned out. One who could not was Lou Criger, but he was not forgotten. He was sent the following proclamation:

WE WANT YOU TO KNOW, OLD PAL, THAT NONE OF US WOULD FORGET YOU, THAT WE WERE ALL THINKING OF YOU AND WE ARE PRAYING FOR YOU AS WE GATHER HERE IN BOSTON FOR ONE MORE TIME TOGETHER. GOD IN HIS WISDOM TO GIVE US OUR BURDENS. YOURS HAS BEEN HEAVY, BUT WE KNOW THAT YOU ARE GIVING IT A GRAND AND GALLANT FIGHT, AND WE KNOW YOU WILL COME THRU, FOR LOU CRIGER HAS ALWAYS FOUGHT IT OUT UNTIL THE LAST STRIKE WAS CALLED. THE ONLY SHADOW ON THE DAY WAS THE FACT THAT YOU CANNOT BE HERE. BUT SINCE YOU COULDN'T BE, YOUR OLD TEAMMATES, AND THE BOYS YOU PLAYED AGAINST, SEND YOU THIS EXPRESSION OF OUR APPRECIATION.

CY YOUNG (RIGHT) AND LOU CRIGER—"NUF CED"
McGREEVEY IS IN THE BACKGROUND.

It was signed by 47 men, ranging from teammates (Cy Young, Candy LaChance, Freddy Parent, Buck Freeman, etc.) to honored foes (Ty Cobb, Big Ed Walsh, Honus Wagner, etc.) to baseball dignitaries (Judge Emil Fuchs) to "Nuf Ced" himself.

No catcher caught more than a 100 or so games in that era, and Criger was no exception. Criger would catch 96 games that season, including all of Young's starts after Farrell sustained an injury in April. Rookie Jake Stahl (40 games) was the primary back-up, but when the ultimate big money games came in October, Lou Criger caught and batted eighth in all eight games of the inaugural World Series, performing, as usual, with great distinction.

CY YOUNG WARMING UP.

CHAPTER 4

AT THE END OF APRIL THE BOSTON AMERICANS WERE 4-6.
THEY CONTINUED TO PLAY WIN-ONE, LOSE-ONE BALL INTO
THE MIDDLE OF MAY, BUT THE GAMES WERE GENERALLY
ENTERTAINING. MURNANE WAS PARTICULARLY TAKEN WITH A
12-5 CONQUEST OF THE NEW YORK HIGHLANDERS ON MAY
9. YOUNG WAS THE WINNING PITCHER IN "A CONTEST FULL
OF ALL THAT GOES TO MAKE THE NATIONAL SPORT INTER-
ESTING," HE INFORMED HIS READERS. THE TEAM MADE A
LITTLE MOVE IN THE LATTER PART OF MAY, EMERGING FROM
THE MONTH WITH A 19-15 RECORD.

The encouraging news was that no one had been able to separate from
the pack. With Long Tom Hughes in good form, and with Buck
Freeman knocking out a pair of two-run homers, the team actually
moved into first place with an 8-2 victory over New York on June 1.
That was the beginning of a three-game sweep and the conclusion of a

successful road trip. They were now embroiled in a very hot pennant race.

In the daily "Baseball Notes," *Globe* readers were informed that "The American League race is by all odds the finest ever known in baseball."

The standings were as follows:

Team	Record
BOSTON	22-15
PHILADELPHIA	22-16
ST. LOUIS	19-14
CHICAGO	20-15
CLEVELAND	17-16
DETROIT	17-19
NEW YORK	15-21
WASHINGTON	10-26

The team to fear was Chicago, at least according to Murnane. "Comiskey's boys can always be counted upon for playing inside baseball and all games to a finish," he observed.

Murnane was placing a lot of emphasis on this coming home stand. "With a long stretch at home vs. the western clubs, Boston should get a good hold on the top rung," he declared, adding that "The home players will receive a warm reception from the friends of the American League, who heretofore have been a little apprehensive about the quality of the goods."

Game one of the home stand went to Boston. "CHICAGO EASY

PREY FOR COLLINS' MEN" headlined the *Globe*. It was game eight of what would stretch into a 11-game winning streak. The push was on.

Murnane's enthusiasm for the club was now beginning to be a universal feeling. "As long as Louie Criger is playing with his present snap and ginger the team will get along without Farrell," declared Jacob Morse in the *Sporting Life*. "It looks as if Collins has come precious near to having four mighty good pitchers, a brace of the best catchers in the land, an infield it would be hard to beat and a powerful trio in the outfield, the whole forming a formidable outfit."

June would be a grand month, as Murnane might say. The Pilgrims/Puritans/Americans would go 19-7, would emerge with a 38-22 record and would not be anywhere other than first place for the remainder of the 1903 season.

July got off to a dramatic start when Cy Young outlasted Chicago's Pat Flaherty in 10 innings, driving in the game's only run himself with a double. The 36-year old legend was very often in the habit of helping out his own cause; he would hit .321 in 1903. (Those 10 innings of play took, by the way, an hour and 30 minutes to complete.)

And nothing was as American in those days (as it was well into the 1970s) as a Fourth of July doubleheader. The Pilgrims rewarded a boisterous crowd with 4-1 and 2-0 triumphs over St. Louis. Pennant fever was raging, as Murnane was there to report, writing that the games were played "before nearly 16,000 people who were as full of enthusiasm as a boy with his first pistol." It turns out there was a reason for that particular analogy, because "the spectators had a lot of satisfaction shooting off revolvers and fireworks when the home team made a good play." That kind of makes a 2003 standing ovation seem pretty tame.

By August that "finest race ever known in baseball" of early June was just about over. Still, of particular interest was a six-game, two-city confrontation with Mack's A's that would begin on August 5 at Philadelphia's ramshackle Columbia Park, where the players still sat on benches, rather than in dugouts, and where the smell of hops, yeast and beer permeated the air (the park was located in a section of Philadelphia known as "Brewerytown"). Big Bill Dinneen shut out the A's and Rube Waddell, 3-0, in the first game. Chief Bender beat Cy Young the following day, and the Boston boys had one more game in Philadelphia in which to make a major statement.

Long Tom Hughes was up to the task, holding the A's down sufficiently while his mates provided impressive offense in an 11-3 victory. Murnane was in high literary gear, proclaiming the game to have been played "for blood and championship honor."

When the Boston boys returned to New England and Huntington Grounds, Dinneen helped them keep the momentum, bagging an emphatic 11-6 victory on August 8.

Philadelphia's problems were mounting, not just because the Pilgrims were looking more and more as if they were the superior team, but their eternally eccentric southpaw star, Rube Waddell, had chosen this inauspicious point in the season to go AWOL (neither for the first time nor the last). Murnane did a little sleuthing and was thus able to explain that "'Rube' is reported to have suggested that Connie and the whole team start for a place considerably farther south than this city."

August 9 was a Sunday, and thus there was no baseball in Boston. So there was more time for fans and the great Tim Murnane to work themselves up for the next game of the series on Monday, August 10. Captain Collins handed the ball to his ace, and Mr. Young pitched admirably while the batters likewise did their jobs. Final score: Boston 7, Philadelphia 2.

There were seven weeks to go, but Murnane was ready to pull the shroud over the defending champs. "More than 10,000 gathered at the American League grounds to see the champion Athletics make another unsuccessful effort to stop the steady march of the Collins brigade toward the championship," enthused Murnane. "Their effort was like running a baby carriage against a locomotive."

Waddell had found his way back to Boston by the 11th, but Hughes was back on the mound for the Americans and he threw another fine game at the A's, beating them by a score of 5-1.

The Philadelphia correspondent of the *Sporting Life* was in a thoroughly conciliatory mood. "That Boston will win the American League pennant is almost assured now," he wrote. "Only a complete collapse of Collins' team could cut down the fine lead of that team, and such a contingency is altogether unlikely at this late stage of the race. If Philadelphia must lose the flag it could go to no worthier city than Boston, which has given its American League club loyal support and has been one of the chief mainstays of the new major league."

Tim Murnane was not about to disagree. After watching the game, he declared that "most every one in the immense crowd was a close follower of the game, and every good point of play was quickly noted and appreciated. In no city in America, with the possible exception of Philadelphia, are the crowds so posted as in Boston."

Boston's notorious penchant for self-congratulation goes way back.

But the truth is that even totally dispassionate observers saw much to like about this team. The balance was superb. The lineup was a dangerous one and the Boston team made all the requisite plays in the field. Parent and Ferris were as good as any middle infield duo in the game (Cy Young had dubbed them "the rabbits" during spring training). LaChance routinely took care of any errant throws. Collins had, quite literally, re-invented the position at third. The outfield was solid, and on the days when Criger was behind the plate, the Boston Americans had a craftsman at work.

The ultimate calling card then, as now, is pitching, and the Pilgrims were living up to Charles Comiskey's spring training prediction that Boston's would be second to none. It began, naturally, with Young, the pitcher's pitcher. He was 36, and his waistline was starting to expand, and there were days when he was quite mortal. But for every off day there were two or three very good ones. He was on his way to a respectable enough 28-10 record.

Young had reached iconic status in the game by 1903, and he was far from finished, even if he was getting a bit on the portly side. He would throw the first twentieth century perfect game in 1904, and he would record the last of his astonishing 511 victories in 1911, when he was 44. He won 75 games after the age of 40. What mattered most was the health of the old soup-bone, as a turn-of-the-century scribe might put it, and the man whose nickname derived from the concept of a cyclone (his real name was Denton True Young, the middle name one of a Civil War general admired by his folks), and at the start of the 1903 season Cy Young still had 160 wins left in his powerful right arm.

"Cy Young is the philosopher of the slab," noted the *Globe's*

Notebook author (almost undoubtedly Murnane himself). "He is thinking all the time, and never sends up a pitch without some definite purpose."

Cy Young preached the simple virtues of a good farm life. Each off-season he trudged back to his Ohio farm where he engaged in all the requisite chores. When he got to spring training, he never needed any mollycoddling; that's for darn sure. Ol' Cy was generally ready to go.

"I never had a sore arm in my life, and I never had my arm rubbed," he declared.

He was immensely strong. In his prime, he would place a baseball in his hand and defy anyone to pull it out. No one could. He lived to a ripe old age (88), and when he died it can be argued he wasn't even sick. No, it was just time; that's all. He expired while sitting in a chair at the home of a Mr. and Mrs. John Benedict, with whom he had lived in the last several years of his life.

Cy Young wasn't just Old School. He *was* the Old School. He came off that Ohio farm in 1890 at age 23 and just sort of took over as the reigning pitcher in baseball. And he surely did it *his* economical way. "I never wasted any time pitching in batting practice or working in the bullpen," he snapped. "Ten warm-up pitches, and I was ready."

Bill Dinneen had been a .500 pitcher the year before, but people who believed in him as being something more than that were now being vindicated. The Syracuse native was the strong, silent type who had been named after famed labor leader Big Bill Haywood and who had defeated the great Cy Young by a 1-0 score the first time he ever

CY YOUNG

laid eyes on him. He was sometimes nicknamed "Redneck," not because of any racist or hayseed propensities, but because, when agitated, he simply boiled in silent rage. He was reluctant to criticize people, but he sure took notes.

His unwillingness to complain about *anything* led to his establishing a phenomenal record in 1904. In that season Bill Dinneen set major league records that, obviously, will never be broken as he went 337 consecutive innings, encompassing 37 complete games, without relief. In that run, during which he went 23-14, were included complete games of 10 innings, two 11s, a 12 and a 16.

In later years he admitted that perhaps pitching that much wasn't such a great idea. "I was a pitcher," he said, "and I would have been a pitcher much longer but for the fact that I had to pitch so often. Only a few men who pitched in those days lasted more than a few years. The strain on their muscles was too much."

Said famed New York writer Joe Williams, "Bill Dinneen was a giant of a man with tremendous power and matchless control."

He was awesomely modest. Asked once to recount his no-hitter against the White Sox, he said, simply, "They had an off day."

He lasted as a pitcher until 1909, whereupon he almost immediately began a distinguished umpiring career that lasted for 27 years. When he retired, he did so as the last person active who had been any kind of participant when the American League was founded in 1901.

He was originally hired to umpire on a highly contingent basis. Said league president Ban Johnson, "I'll let you finish the season, and we'll see what kind of an umpire you are."

The experiment lasted 27 seasons, and when it was over Johnson's successor Will Harridge said, "If there ever was a finer umpire, especially on balls and strikes, than Dinneen, I don't know who he was."

But all that was in the unknown future for Bill Dinneen. He was en route to a 21-win season, and he was setting himself up to become the first great World Series hero, even if he had no way of knowing it.

The third primary starter was Long Tom Hughes, who provided a nice personality balance to the taciturn Dinneen. Keeping still was not his style.

His unofficial nickname was "Goat-getter." According to one contemporary appraisal, Hughes "comments on their habits, their facial adornments and any other unkind things that comes into his mind." He got a lot of mileage out of a story that he had once signed a contract with an "X," leading some to believe that he was illiterate. The truth is that he had a broken knuckle on his right hand at the time and he thought it would be amusing to sign the "X" and set people's tongues wagging.

He spent 13 years in the big leagues, but 1903 was by far his best season, in part because he never seemed to take anything about himself too seriously. Collins had picked him up from the Baltimore squad in 1902. His arm was sore, but there was something about the 6-1 right-hander that appealed to the Boston skipper. Perhaps the captain recalled the day in 1901 when the rookie hurler had defeated Dinneen, then with the Boston Nationals, 1-0 in 17 innings.

He certainly had his career moments. He would go 20-7 for the '03 Sox and he threw five complete-game shutouts for the 1905 Washington Senators. But he was 131-174 lifetime and perhaps the reason can best be summed up by a 1912 critique: "A happy-go-lucky person who takes no particular care of himself, smokes cigarettes like a streamer when things are hot and other things when they are cold."

Baseball history is laden with such characters, and it is also laden with examples of journeymen players who had that one golden season. The 1903 campaign was Long Tom Hughes' brush with baseball glory.

August rolled into September with the Boston Americans giving everyone the back of their hands. After defeating Detroit on August 15, Jimmy Collins was moved to new heights of bravado. According to Tim Murnane, "Capt. Collins said after the game that the series settles the pennant fight, and that none of the clubs can now beat Boston."

He was merely dealing in reality. In one stretch they won 15 of 19 road games, this in an era when to go on the road was to enter truly hostile physical conditions, and all manner of conceivable chicanery on the part of the home side.

As far as anyone knew, the season would end on September 28. The Boston Pilgrims/Puritans/Americans were playing to win the American League pennant, and that was that. A challenge for a post-season series from the Boston Nationals issued on August 18 had been quickly rejected. What would the Americans, comfortably stocked with the best players the Nationals once had to offer, possibly gain from a series with a sixth-place club?

On September 1, however, a tiny story, located beneath the box score of the day-before Cleveland-St. Louis game, cropped up in the sports section of the *Boston Globe*.

SERIES OF GAMES

Killilea Will Soon Confer with Dreyfuss Regarding
Boston-Pittsburg Match

MILWAUKEE, Wis. Sept 1—Henry Killilea, owner of the Boston club, will meet Barney Dreyfuss, owner of the Pittsburg club of the National League, in a few days, and endeavor to arrange for a series of games this fall between the winning teams of the two major leagues, and play for the championship of the United States.

Mr. Killilea does not care to talk about the terms under which the games will be played at this time, as he deems it best to see Mr. Dreyfuss first and get his views on the matter. Games may be played in New York, Pittsburg, Boston and Chicago.

It was the first mention of what would become the World Series, and it is interesting to note that it came in the form of a team-to-team challenge involving owners, not a league-to-league challenge involving presidents.

CHAPTER 5

CAPTAIN COLLINS WAS ECSTATIC. HE COULD THINK OF NO
MORE STIMULATING IDEA IN LIFE THAN THAT OF HE AND HIS
BOYS TAKING ON THE CHAMPIONS OF THE NATIONAL
LEAGUE.

There had been no such confrontation throughout the nineties, when a shakedown period left professional baseball with just one major league, the National. There was a post-season competition called the Temple Cup, which matched the first and second-place teams. It never really piqued the cranks' interest.

This was real competition, the way it had been when the National League champions annually played the American Association titlist every year from 1884 to 1891. Acknowledging that the details had to be worked out and that there indeed remained the formality of his team clinching the pennant, Collins nevertheless reacted with glee to the concept of a World Series in the September 3 editions of all the papers.

"Boston is ready for such a series," he declared. "I am confident that if we played those games now Pittsburg would never get a look in. I won't say how many of the games we will win if we play, but you can put it down in black and white that we will get the majority. I think we have the better team in every branch."

Pittsburg (there was no "h" attached in those days) was the two-time defending National League champion. In 1902 the team, only occasionally known as the "Pirates," had finished 27-1/2 games ahead of runner-up Brooklyn, a record margin that still stands. The team was somewhat less overpowering in '03—they would defeat New York by 6-1/2 games—but it was still the class of the National League, and it still had the great John Peter (Honus) Wagner, a remarkably versatile player who could play any position on the diamond other than pitcher and who had just been moved full-time to shortstop, where he remains the most acclaimed player in the position's history. No less an authority than John McGraw would go to his grave 29 years later swearing that Wagner had been the greatest all-around player of them all—greater than Ty Cobb, greater than Babe Ruth, greater than *anybody*.

The Pirates were owned by Barney Dreyfuss, a man of enormous stature in the game. By all the standards of the day the Pittsburg team was regarded as a class organization, and the very idea that a Dreyfuss team would challenge *them* conferred immediate status on the Boston American League baseball club.

While his owner negotiated the details of the post-season series with Mr. Dreyfuss, Collins kept his team focused on its play. He hadn't

Pittsburg Pirates owner Barney Dreyfuss

JOHN PETER "HONUS" WAGNER

tolerated any sloppy performance in the months of April, May, June, July and August, so there was no reason to sanction any shenanigans now that his squad would be preparing for the biggest series of its life.

Schedules were a bit different in those days. Collins' team played its final road game in New York on September 8, losing to the Highlanders by a 1-0 score when Buck Freeman fouled off 10 pitches before flying out deep to right field with two away in the ninth. The team made good use of the home field the next day by taking two from Washington, despite Freeman being ejected in the first game for "giving cheap talk to the umpire."

The pennant march continued the following day with a 3-0 victory over the Senators. "Uncle Cyrus limited them to three hits," is the way Tim Murnane framed it. Freeman's two-run home run had PUT THE GAME ON ICE, according to a headline.

Buck Freeman was just 5'9" and 170 pounds, but no man in early twentieth century baseball hit the ball consistently harder. "'Buck' is the champion long-distance hitter of the country," Murnane wrote. "The echo that went swelling around the park after 'Buck' met that ball sounded like the bark of a mastiff at the dead of night in a big barn when some one steps on his tail."

No one has ever described a Barry Bonds homer like that.

Murnane went on to lavish praise on Ferris ("an extra fine game at second"), Young ("doubtful if 'Cy' Young ever had more speed than yesterday") and just about everyone on both sides, saying the game was "full of ginger." He liked the direction in which Capt. Collins had his team heading. "Boston is still battling for every game in sight, with no let up for that pennant," Murnane concluded.

There was no countdown and no one had yet coined the phrase "magic number." So it was that on the morning of September 17 Bostonians awoke to discover a very important development had taken place.

The pennant race was officially over.

The story began: "The Boston American league team has 13 scheduled and postponed games yet to play, and Cleveland now has 11. Therefore, Boston can lose all, making 56 lost, and Cleveland can win all, making 83 won. This would give Boston the championship, as it would have won the same number of games as Cleveland, and have lost one less, as follows:

Team	*Won*	*Lost*	*Pc Won*
BOSTON	*83*	*56*	*.597*
CLEVELAND	*83*	*57*	*.593*

As Tony Soprano would say, "End of story."

That was the morning paper. The evening edition got right to the point, saying, "By clipping the Cleveland wings yesterday, the Boston Americans became champions after a well-fought campaign."

The score had been 14-7. Long Tom Hughes was the winner. Chick Stahl had gone 5-for-5. The Americans had accomplished the extraordinarily rare feat of scoring in all eight available at-bats.

According to the *Globe,* "The Boston players were out for the game, and the Cleveland boys were soon impressed with the fact Collins' men were no counterfeit champions, but ball players from the ground up, good for a full season's work, and the gamiest bunch now playing ball.

"Boston was bound to win the game and settle this championship once and for all and pushed the clever Cleveland team to one side like so much driftwood—phenomenal Larry (the great Napoleon "Larry" Lajoie) and all."

Yeah!

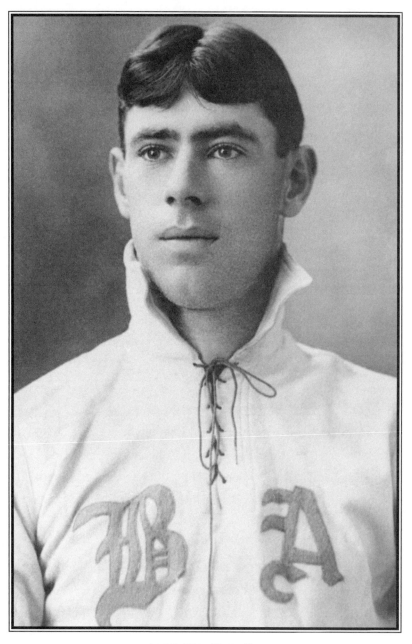

LONG TOM HUGHES

Chapter 6

Collins the Captain and manager, as opposed to
Collins the nonpareil third baseman, had been phe-
nomenally fortunate. Aside from the loss of the
Duke of Marlboro in the very first week, his team
had been blessedly free of injury.

Day after day after day he was able to count on the presence of both his entire preferred infield and two-thirds of his starting outfield (Chick Stahl did miss half the season and John O'Brien was needed to fill in). His core pitchers were always available. There is no more comforting thought for a manager than that of having his best players readily available.

The skipper was going to have his center fielder ready for the World Series, but by the third week of September no one was certain there was even going to be a World Series. Few things worthwhile ever come easy in life, and the negotiations were not proceeding smoothly. How many games? Where would they be played; i.e., how many in Boston and how many in Pittsburg? And, most importantly, as always, there was the matter of finances. How would the money be split up?

Dreyfuss was being more accommodating to the players. The gracious Pittsburg owner, a superb combination of businessman/sportsman, said he wanted to pull off this National League-American League series as long as "it is good for the players." He said he was quite willing to give 100 percent of the proceeds to the players. Henry Killilea was not quite that magnanimous. He was thinking more along the lines of 50-50.

Dreyfuss was operating at an advantage. The contracts of the Pittsburg players ran until October 15. But the contracts of the Boston players expired on September 30, which actually gave the players some leverage.

When Collins passed along the word to the Boston players of the discrepancy between the two management viewpoints, they were not highly agitated. "The players yelled murder," Collins told reporters, "and it was useless to argue with them. They wanted all the receipts at first, but finally agreed to tell Killilea they would play for 75 percent."

American League president Ban Johnson intervened, and the split between management and players was set at 60-40 in favor of the players.

The agreement was enacted and signed on September 16, but not announced to the public for 10 days. But for all anyone knows the final agreement may have been back-dated, for the following story appeared in the *Globe* of September 24, eight days after the official contract date and two days before it was announced to the public.

Players Protest

Some Objections to the Business Manager Sharing in Receipts of the Post-Season Series

The final arrangements for the post-season series between Boston and Pittsburg have not been completed, and while manager Smart (Business Manager Joseph Smart) and Capt. Collins refused to give out anything official, the fact is that some of the players have protested against the business manager being counted in the division.

Mr. Smart has in no way signified his desire to share in the rake-off, but Pres. Killilea thought he was entitled to do so the same was as other salaried men.

Mr. Killilea may have to come here and fix up matters (he resided in Milwaukee). As Lou Criger has informed friends that he will leave for home at the close of his contract, and one or two other men have hinted that they will do the same.

The whole business should be left in the hands of the owners and Capt. Collins.

The chances however, are that the games will be played.

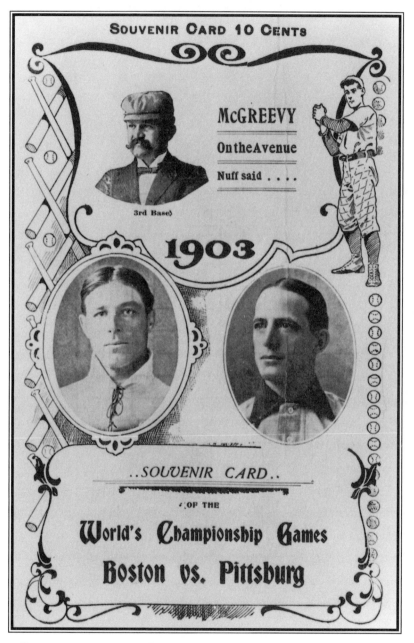

SOUVENIR CARD FROM BOSTON'S HUNTINGTON AVENUE GROUNDS
FOR THE FIRST WORLD SERIES.

CHAPTER 7

For when the announcement was finally made on September 26 that there would be a series for "the championship of the world" between Boston and Pittsburg, it was made clear that the business manager of the Boston Americans had played a pivotal role in arranging the confrontation.

According to the *Globe*, "The players wanted to play the games, but thought they were entitled to more than Mr. Killilea offered, and Manager Smart deserves great credit for the interest he has taken in the matter and for finally bringing about a settlement of what was at one time a serious affair. He knew the public was anxious to see the games and so worked hard to bring about a meeting of the teams."

Ban Johnson had made his feelings known, as well. The American League president had dispatched a telegram to Captain Collins, as follows: "The press and public demand the games, and you should impress this fact upon your players."

So let the gamesmanship begin. Cooed the Boston skipper, "It looks as if those stories from Pittsburg about the poor condition of the teams were for the purpose of letting the Dreyfuss boys down easy."

The final agreement itself was straightforward enough, and here it is, questionable punctuation and all:

It is hereby agreed by and between Pittsburg Club of the National League and the Boston American League Club of the American League as follows:

1,– That a post season series shall be played between said base ball clubs consisting of a series of 9 games, if it be necessary to play that number before either club should win 5 games, said series however to terminate when either club shall win 5 games.

2,– Said games to be played at the following times and places: At Boston, Mass., Oct. 1, 2, & 3 (Thursday, Friday and Saturday). At Pittsburg, Pa., [Oct.] 5, 6, 7 & 8 (Monday, Tuesday, Wednesday and Thursday). At Boston, Mass., [Oct.] 10 and 12 (Saturday and Monday); providing however, in the event of the weather being such as to prevent a game being played on either of said days, such game shall be postponed until the next succeeding day when the weather will permit such game to be played at the city where scheduled. And in that event there shall be a moving back of the aforesaid schedule for the day or days lost on account of said inclement weather.

3,– Each club shall bear the expense of the games played on their respective grounds, excepting the expense of umpire.

4,– Each club shall furnish and pay the expenses of one umpire to officiate during said series and it is agreed that the umpire so agreed upon to be furnished shall be O'Day from the National League and Connelly from the American League.

4½ No player to participate who was not a regular member of team Sep 1, 1903.

5,– The minimum price of admission in each city shall be 50 [cents] and the visiting club shall be settled with by being paid 25 [cents] for every admission ticket sold.

6,– A statement to be furnished the visiting club after each game, final settlement to be at the close of the series.

The respective captains of each team shall meet with the umpires above designated before the beginning of the series to agree upon a uniform interpretation of the playing rules.

IN WITNESS WHEREOF the parties hereto have caused these presents to be signed by their respective Presidents this 16 day of September, A.D. 1903.

In Presence of   PITTSBURG ATHLETIC CO.

                                          by   [Barney Dreyfuss signature]

                                                    President.

BOSTON AMERICAN LEAGUE CLUB

                                          by   [Henry J. Killilea signature]

                                                    President.

It is hereby agreed by and between Pittsburg Club of the National League and the Boston American League Club of the American League as follows:

1,- That a post season series shall be played between said base ball clubs consisting of a series of 9 games, if it be necessary to play that number before either club should win 5 games, said series however to terminate when either club shall win 5 games.

2,- Said games to be played at the following times and places: At Boston, Mass., Oct. 1, 2, & 3 (Thursday, Friday and Saturday) At Pittsburg, Pa., " 5, 6, 7 & 8 (Monday, Thuesday, Wednesday and Thursday) At Boston, Mass., " 10 and 12 (Saturday and Monday); providing however, in the event of the weather being such as to prevent a game being played on either of said days, such game shall be postponed until the next succeeding day when the weather will permit such game to be played at the city where scheduled. And in that event there shall be a moving back of the aforesaid schedule for the day or days lost on account of said inclement weather.

3,- Each club shall bear the expense of the games played on their respective grounds, excepting the expense of umpire.

4,- Each club shall furnish and pay the expenses of one umpire to officiate during said series and it is agreed that the umpire so agreed upon to be furnished shall be O'Day from the National League and Connelly from the American League.

4½ no player to participate who was not a regular member of team Sep 1, 1903.

5,- The minimum price of admission in each city shall be 50 cts. and the visiting club shall be settled with by being paid 25 cts. for every admission ticket sold.

6,- A statement to be furnished the visiting club after each game, final settlement to be at the close of the series.

The respective captains of each team shall meet with the umpires above designated before the beginning of the series to agree upon a uniform interpretation of the playing rules.

IN WITNESS WHEREOF the parties hereto have caused these presents to be signed by their respective Presidents this 16 day of September, A. D. 1903.

In Presence Of

PITTSBURGH ATHLETIC CO.
by _Barney Dreyfuss_
President.
BOSTON AMERICAN LEAGUE BALL CLUB
by _Henry J. Killilea_
President.

FACSIMILE OF THE ORIGINAL AGREEMENT TO STAGE THE FIRST WORLD SERIES.

One thing jumps out at a twenty-first century reader. The date for player eligibility, September 1, has remained constant for a century.

Umpiring was always a touchy matter in those rough-and-tumble days. Each team had been asked for its recommendations, and the Americans had put forth the names of Tom Connolly (note the spelling in the above agreement) and Silk O'Loughlin, described by the *Globe* as "a good, nervy pair."

Ban Johnson was, of course, delighted. "The baseball public demanded the games," he declared, "and the American League is trying to please the public."

The cranks in both cities were the happiest people of all. Almost immediately, the Royal Rooters announced plans to visit Pittsburg. "The 'royal rooters' will accompany the Boston team to Pittsburg and give Collins' boys the encouragement they can, as they did the Boston National team in Baltimore in 1897," the *Globe* explained. The party would be over 200 strong.

There was equal fervor in Pittsburg, where an expatriate Boston pitcher named A.J. Pratt, now a Pittsburg businessman, was making plans to lead a contingent of Pittsburg backers to Boston. Said the *Globe* on the morning of September 27: "A special train with the rooters who are willing and ready to lose their lungs and money in defense of Pittsburg and Boston, will leave here (Pittsburg) Tuesday night and reach Boston late Wednesday afternoon."

Pratt delighted in pointing out that he had not been in Boston for 31 years, and that the last time he was in town he had pitched an 11-inning game.

In addition, the *Globe* told us that John Newell, "famous as a hotel man," would be taking a "carload of friends and a box of coin to Boston." Yet another car was to be headed up by Alderman Steve Toole, "the once-famous Brooklyn pitcher," and still another was in the custody of Frank Hathaway, a bookmaker who would be carrying "half a thousand friends of the turf."

In another development, *Globe* readers were informed that in Carnegie, Pa. a "Wagner Club" was being organized and would go to Boston Tuesday night just to see that their old pal and fellow townsman Hans "gets the hot end of nothing."

THE GREAT HONUS WAGNER

CHAPTER 8

THIS WAS NO NFL-AFL SITUATION, CIRCA 1969. THE
AMERICAN LEAGUE HAD SPRUNG ONTO THE SCENE AS A
COMPLETELY VIABLE COMPETITOR FROM THE DAY OF ITS
FIRST SET OF GAMES IN 1901. ONLY A NATIONAL LEAGUE
HARDHEAD COULD FAIL TO RECOGNIZE THE FACTS, THE
MOST OBVIOUS OF WHICH WAS THAT OF THE 182 AMERICAN
LEAGUE PLAYERS IN THAT 1901 SEASON, 111 OF THEM
HAD COME FROM THE NATIONAL LEAGUE OF 1900.

And we're not just talking about subs or fringe players, either. We're talking about people such as Jimmy Collins and Cy Young, the two key players on the Boston team. The National League owners were being forced to pay the price for their monopolistic and penurious ways.

The Pittsburg club had an aura left over from its stunning march through the National League in 1902 (a 27-1/2 game romp, remember), but this was not quite the same overpowering baseball machine in 1903. The New York Highlanders of the American League had marched in and stolen away pitchers Jack Chesbro and Jesse Tannehill, a staunch pair of hurlers who had gone a combined 48-12 in 1902, and the Pirates had not been able to find a satisfactory replacement, not that anyone could.

As the regular season drew to a close and each team began to make its preparations, both physical and mental, for the upcoming clash, the news out of Pittsburg was all bad. In the September 19 edition of the *Sporting Life* Jacob Morse had informed his readers that the Pittsburg situation was so dire that there may be no World Series because the National League team is in such a "crippled" situation it may be compelled to decline. The Pirates had been scuffling on the mound (or, as they would have said themselves, "in the box") all season, and they did not need any complications heading into the World Series. But the sad truth was that 16-game winner Ed Doheny was a perpetually tormented soul, and with two weeks remaining in the season he suffered a serious mental breakdown and had to be institutionalized. He never pitched again. He was in and out of institutions for the rest of his life, dying in 1916 a month after his 32nd birthday.

Number two starter Sam Leever was having his own problems, having injured his right (throwing) shoulder while trapshooting, a very popular activity of the day. Player-manager Fred Clarke had a great deal to worry about, and the news got even worse, when, a few days before the Series, it was reported that star third baseman Tommy Leach was a doubtful participant because he was suffering from possible blood poisoning in the middle finger of his throwing hand. He had attempted to perform his own impromptu surgery the previous Saturday by taking a knife to a pimple he had discovered that morning. Moreover, the great Honus Wagner had leg woes of one kind or another, and legs were a vital part of the Dutchman's all-encompassing game.

Pre-Series coverage was very much like it would be today. On the day before the Series, for example, the *Globe*—which is to say, the great Tim Murnane—gave its readers an exhaustive position-by-position comparison.

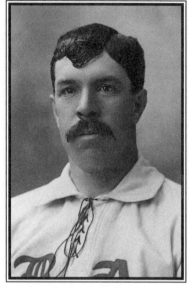

KITTY BRANSFIELD   CANDY LACHANCE

FIRST BASEMEN

Pittsburg—*Kitty Bransfield.*

Boston—*Candy LaChance.*

"In Bransfield and LaChance we find very little choice...they will probably come out the series with honors about even up."

CLAUDE (MEINIE) RITCHIE

HOBE FERRIS

SECOND BASEMEN

Pittsburg—*Claude (Meinie) Ritchie.*

Boston—*Hobe Ferris.*

"Ritchie is not aggressive as Ferris, and will have to hump himself to come out of the present series with as good a record as the Boston youngster."

TOMMY LEACH

JIMMY COLLINS & JOHN SULLIVAN

THIRD BASEMEN

Pittsburg—*Tommy Leach.*

Boston—*Jimmy Collins.*

*"Capt. Collins has a lively young opponent in Tommy
Leach. . . Collins is a better batsman than Leach and
has the Pittsburg man cinched as a fielder. . . Leach
will take chances and make remarkable plays, but will
not class with the great Collins when the series is over."*

HONUS WAGNER

FREDDY PARENT

SHORTSTOP

Pittsburg—*Honus Wagner.*

Boston—*Freddy Parent.*

*"It may seem ridiculous to mention Fred Parent in the
same day with the great Wagner, but Boston will take a
chance on the small man from Maine. Wagner has no
weakness and the same may be said of Parent. Wagner's
great reach gives him the advantage over the Boston
man, and while we all tip our caps to Mr. Wagner as a
winning ball player, Freddie Parent is about the next
best shortstop to tie up to."*

FRED CLARKE

PAT DOUGHERTY

LEFT FIELDERS

Pittsburg—*Fred Clarke.*

Boston—*Pat Dougherty.*

"In left field Fred Clarke has Dougherty outclassed as a fielder. The Boston man is the better batsman and run-getter. Both are game to the quick, and I look for these two men to do effective work in the coming series.

GINGER BEAUMONT   CHICK STAHL

CENTER FIELDERS

Pittsburg—*Ginger Beaumont.*

Boston—*Chick Stahl.*

"In center Stahl has Beaumont beaten as a fielder. The Pittsburg man has several points on Chick on bunting and run getting. Both have shown up well when called upon for great ball playing, and no one need fear for the Boston man as a stayer."

JIMMY SEBRING

BUCK FREEMAN

RIGHT FIELDERS

Pittsburg—*Jimmy Sebring.*

Boston—*Buck Freeman.*

"Boston has much the better of it in right field, as Freeman is the hardest hitter playing ball, and can field fully as well as Sebring. The young Pittsburg (21 years old) outfielder has made good in the league, and will no doubt show up well in the coming series, but Buck Freeman has all the box artists worried when they face him, and before the show is over will have done much more damage than Sebring."

CATCHERS

Pittsburg—*Ed (Chink) Phelps, Harry Smith.*

Boston—*Lou Criger, Charley Farrell.*

"Boston has in Criger the prince of catchers. He out-classes Phelps, who is perhaps as good a man for the position as there is in the league. Criger has the nerve, and gives his team confidence. Phelps is a good young-ster and a better batsman than the Boston man. Criger can stop the base running for any club, as Pittsburg will find...Farrell is a much more valuable man than Smith, should either be called on. Farrell is a grand hitter, while Smith is weak. Farrell makes a grand coach for the pitchers and has the weak points of the Pittsburg boys down fine. For example, he would keep them high for Wagner, low for Leach, high for Bransfield, high for Clarke, Ritchey and Phelps, and high for Beaumont. That would handicap the league players and hitting would be light."

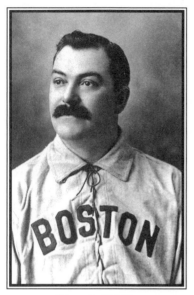

CHARLEY FARRELL

LOU CRIGER

EDWARD PHELPS

PITCHERS

Pittsburg—*Deacon Phillippe,*
Sam Leever, Brickyard Kennedy.

Boston—*Cy Young,*
Bill Dinneen, Long Tom Hughes.

"In Young, Dinneen and Hughes Boston has the finest
string of pitchers ever under contract to one ball team.
Man for man, they can out-pitch the Pittsburgers, and
right here is where Boston has the best of the meeting.
Not one of the Pittsburg men has been tested with real
fire. Leever has shown good headwork and has a fine
break to his ball, while the world knows what Cy
Young can do when wound up for the money. Dinneen
can outpitch Phillippe while Hughes can outpitch any
one of the bunch at times and his friends are banking
on him being fit for the big trial this week."

DEACON PHILLIPPE

CY YOUNG

LONG TOM HUGHES

BILL DINNEEN

Though the language is somewhat Victorian, the baseball thoughts could have come directly from Bill James. Look at the catching comment, for example. James aficionados recall how often he harped on the need to "cut off the running game" in one of his team treatises. And so Lou Criger, we read, "can stop the base-running for any club, as Pittsburg will find." Is there, likewise, any doubt that Tim Murnane believed pitching to be baseball's most important asset? Joe Torre would hardly disagree.

In a journalistic custom that persists to this day, Murnane sought the opinion of a "well-posted baseball man," whom he promised anonymity, on the subject of the team match-ups.

His analysis:

"Collins' aggregation has been playing stiffer teams, has been fighting to win and is at the top of its game. Since June the pitchers have been strong, the men have accorded grand support, the outfield has done well as a whole and the team has maintained a good standard in batting, until now they have become well-nigh invincible.

"How much different are the conditions with Pittsburg. Here's a team which has long since reached its highest standard of play and has gone back. Its ranks have been broken by several strong pitchers going to the other league. For two years its fighting blood has hardly been aroused and its players are in poor condition.

"Individual comparisons count for little in getting a line on the results of these games, but with well-matched pitchers, team work and hitting will win, bearing in mind that the luck of baseball upsets all calculations at times.

"Boston undoubtedly has a more reliable throwing catcher. The infields are both naturally fast and sure, but Boston is at a disadvantage in right and left field. Both Freeman and Dougherty are weak in catching hard hit fly balls on the run and the latter is often unable to judge them. This weakness against the Pittsburg team may prove costly. And let me say right here that Pittsburg is easily whipped unless they have on their batting togs.

"On paper today, Boston's pitching talent stands second to none. The men are universally considered strong in the box. This feeling arises from this year's success. A year ago would they have been so greatly favored in comparison with Pittsburg, even omitting Chesbro and Tannehill?

"At the beginning of this series the determination to win, team work and ability to hit will be evident in both teams. But the boys of the Smoky City are in a rut, and the question is how long will it take in these games to key them up to a standard of play equal to that of Collins' team?

"No none would deny that they are not capable of it. Disregarding the final result I predict that Pittsburg will win a larger percentage of the last four games than of the first four unless Series proves, as some of the Temple cup series have, a walkover.

"After figuring it all out the best way to enjoy yourself is to go and see the games the last three days of this week."

St. Louis Browns manager Jimmy McAleer was keen on the Americans. "That Boston infield," he said, "has been playing wonderful ball against us all season, and I can't figure Pittsburg winning."

One John Keenan, identified only as a "keen observer" who had been monitoring the National League all season, had this to say: "I think that Pittsburg will take more chances and will be alive to every opening. They will, however, have trouble in hitting the Boston pitchers, and must earn most of their runs by short hits. Boston will have the worst of it with the crowd on the field, and rules allowing three bases for hits over the ropes. Collins' boys have won many games this season with a timely home run, and have the finest bunch of long-distance hitters in the business in Freeman, Collins, Parent and the two Stahls, and the finest hitter in the business for runs in Dougherty. While I should pick Boston, I see no reason why the thing is not an even-up game all around."

As one might guess, the Pittsburg viewpoint was somewhat different. The *Sporting Life's* Pittsburg correspondent A.A. Cratty was skeptical. "The writer has never seen the Boston Americans at work," he said, "but one who watched the nine combat the Cleveland team in the latter's city some time in the spring said he didn't care much for their display."

Business Manager Smart revealed himself to be a fiery partisan. "It will be a case of take them to the hospital after Boston is through with the Dreyfuss outfit. I can't see how any team in the business has a look-in with Collins' men at present, and Pittsburg must show me," he harrumphed.

Reporting from Boston, the *Sporting Life's* Jacob Morse said, simply, "Everyone here is agog for the Pittsburg series."

Money and betting was never far from anyone's mind a century ago. "Some friends of the National League in Boston favor Pittsburg," Murnane observed, "but when it comes to betting anything more than a bottle of cologne the Pittsburg admirers usually demand big odds."

A Pittsburg "sporting man" named Alec Moore did telegraph a Boston friend just before the Series, saying "Hear that you have money in Boston to put up at two to one on your favorites. If so, let me know, and I will furnish you with all you want."

There was a reply: "Stop squealing. Be a good sport and bring all your money to Boston, where you can place it at even up, which should be good betting."

CHAPTER 9

IF PEOPLE THINK WE ARE A SPORTS-CRAZED SOCIETY,
THERE IS A GOOD REASON. IT IS CLEARLY IN OUR GENES.

The 1903 World Series did not exactly sneak up on the citizens of Boston and New England. There was neither radio nor television, but newspapers were up to the task of informing the citizenry.

With both the searing prose of the writers and the blazing wit and superb artistry of the sports cartoonists—the demise of the sports cartoon in the daily American newspaper is one of the sad casualties of the late twentieth century—the newspapers alerted both the passionate cranks and the more measured casually interested followers of sport that something very special was going to take place at the Huntington Avenue Grounds on the afternoon of Thursday, October 1, 1903.

The game that afternoon was the lead story of the morning *Globe,* complete with a huge, simple, direct headline:

READY TO BATTLE FOR THE WORLD'S CHAMPIONSHIP

It was accompanied by a very detailed cartoon depicting the Boston side defending a beachhead against invading pirates.

"Both teams are in the pink of condition, and a battle royal may be looked for," Murnane advised. "For three years the friends of the National and American leagues have longed to see the champions come together, but it was reserved for Boston to have the honor and pleasure of witnessing the first game."

Murnane had covered the Americans' workout at their ballpark the day before and reported that "the boys took plenty of batting practice and claimed nothing could bother them in the way of a pitched ball."

As far as Boston's own hurling was concerned, Capt. Collins took the occasion to make an announcement he could have made on April 1: Cy Young would have the honor of being the first man to take the mound in a proper twentieth century World Series. "All right," cracked Cy, "I will try to be there."

The Pittsburg team had arrived the day before the game and had set up headquarters at the Hotel Vendome. After a lunch, many of the players had gone across the river to see a football game between Harvard and Bowdoin.

One matter of interest was Tommy Leach's damaged finger. He'd reported that the finger was healing and he would indeed be in the lineup. Asked for his thoughts on the Series, the third-sacker demurred.

"You see, it's not up to me to have much to say," he replied. "You had better see Mr. Dreyfuss or Mr. Clarke. They'll tell you all about it."

Having said that, Leach proceeded to tell the Boston press all about it himself.

"I think we have it all over them," he said. "I don't see how we can lose. I know the Boston Americans are in the upper class as a ball team, and nobody but a lunatic would deny that. Still, we have been playing together for a long time and our pitchers are all in shape. The Boston Americans will realize that they are up against the toughest proposition yet when they stack up against Pittsburg. It will be fight from the drop of the hat, and no doubt the better team will win the series."

The press corps did catch up with Pirates' owner Barney Dreyfuss, and he did have something to say. "I've come all the way from the West to see my boys take two out of three here," he declared. "I do not underrate the Boston Americans, but I do think the Pittsburg team has something on them. Of course, I've had a wrong guess before, but I do think candidly and truly that the Pittsburg team is the best in the country, and I know that right here in Boston you have one, too."

Player-manager Clarke, every bit as revered in the Smoke City as Captain Collins was in the Hub, was never one for braggadocio. But neither was he one to sidestep an issue. "All I care to say is that I never went into a game yet that I did not expect to win," he said. "You can say that we will be in the game heads, hands and feet tomorrow."

As always, wagering was on everyone's mind. Remarking that Collins had laughed at a supposed Clarke prediction that the Pirates would sweep the Series by saying, "We will pick up a few games, all right," Murnane added, "And this is how the Boston sports think, for there was an army of them around yesterday looking for Pittsburg money, but there was little to be found." Continued Murnane, unable to resist being parochial, "Many believe that the Pittsburg people want to get a line on the Boston team before laying down their coin. In Pittsburg all they know about Boston is what they have read, and reading a Pittsburg paper is a poor way to learn of Boston's good points."

Elsewhere in the paper, it was reported that the unofficial odds were 10 to 8 in favor of Boston. This was primarily based on the words of "a well-dressed young man" who had called at the Hotel Vendome the night before and who had "produced a big roll of money." He had asked to see the Pittsburg rooters who had accompanied the team and was told they had gone to the theatre.

He told intermediaries he would be present at the ballpark on the afternoon of Game 1 with a bankroll of $10,000 and would put it on Boston at odds of 10 to 8. He said he would be found in the third row of the grandstand, that he would wear a pink flower in the lapel of his coat and would accommodate anyone that had money to place against Boston.

In other news, the Royal Rooters were finalizing plans for their trip to Pittsburg. Their intention was to be on the same Sunday morning train the team had booked to Pittsburg, unless "the number is great to take a special train." The round-trip train cost was $20, and on the morning of Game 1 100 people had already signed up. Prospective travelers were reminded that when the Rooters had gone to Baltimore five years previous it had been "the time of their lives."

Clarke himself had been one of many Pittsburg players nursing an injury as the team stumbled home in the final three weeks, but he was not going to allow that to be a potential excuse in case his team were to get in trouble during the World Series. According to Tim Murnane, Clarke said that "his cripples, so much advertised, will appear in first-class shape and be ready to fight to the bitter end. He hopes that Collins' men will be in as good a shape as his men are."

Fred Clifford Clarke was one of the towering figures in baseball's early days. Born on October 3, 1872, in Winterset, Kansas, he remained a classic Man of the Plains his entire life. While still an active player, he purchased a property (called "The Little Pirate Ranch") in Winfield, Kansas and lived on it until he died in 1960. In a 1910 article it was written that "In Winfield, an invitation to the Clarke estate is looked forward to and hoped for by every one of the native farmers, for they know Fred's hospitality."

Men were drawn to Fred Clarke, so much so that Barney Dreyfuss, approximately the last man on earth anyone would label "impulsive," entrusted his ball club to the precocious outfielder before Fred Clarke had even turned 25. That's correct; long before Bucky Harris, Lou Boudreau or Dave DeBusschere, there was Fred Clarke, manager of Dreyfuss' Louisville (and later Pittsburg) ball club in the 1897 season at the age of 24 years, 8 months and 28 days.

He was indeed known then as the "Boy Manager." But it did not take long for Fred Clarke to demonstrate the wisdom of Barney Dreyfuss. When the National League shrank from 12 to 8 teams following the 1899 season, one of the casualties was Louisville. But Dreyfuss immediately resurfaced in Pittsburg, and brought with him stalwarts such as Clarke and Honus Wagner. The Pirates won the National League pennant in both 1901 and 1902, and the latter club must be included in any serious discussion concerning the greatest teams of all time. As previously stated, they won the race by a record 27-½ games, anchored by the starting rotation of Jack Chesbro (28-6,

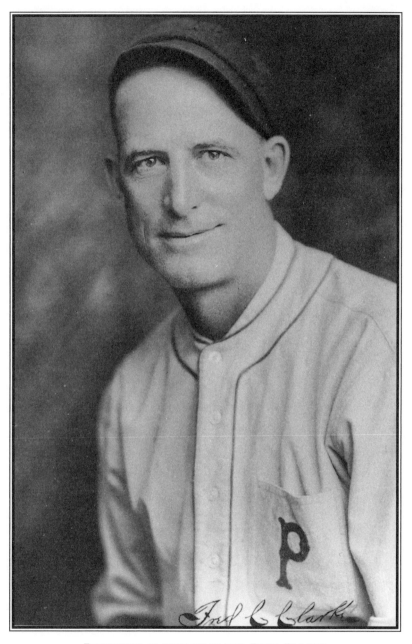

PITTSBURG PLAYER-MANAGER FRED CLARKE

2.17), Deacon Phillippe (20-9, 2.05) and Jesse Tannehill (20-6, 1.95), backed by Sam Leever (16-7, 2.39) and Ed Doheny (16-6, 2.53).

As a manager Clarke was described in the *Biographical Dictionary of American Sports* as "an energetic, aggressive, inspirational leader," who stressed "conditioning, practice, dedication and desire."

Frederick Lieb, who covered baseball for more than 60 years, described Clarke as a "fighting bobcat." Maintained Lieb, "with the possible exception of (Ty) Cobb and John McGraw, baseball never knew a sturdier competitor than Clarke. As a player-manager, he gave the fans, and his employer, Barney Dreyfuss, everything he had, every hour of the day."

Fred Clarke was a great player, a .312 lifetime hitter who went into the Hall of Fame in 1945. Few players ever made such an instant splash: he was 5-for-5 in his debut on June 30, 1894. Equally proficient on offense or defense, he was also a serious thinker. Fred Clarke pioneered the idea of sunglasses for ballplayers.

Writing in *Baseball Magazine,* one William H. Locke had this to say, "As a manager, Fred Clarke is really better than as a player. He has one motto; there are not many words in it. It is: 'Get results.' There are two means of getting results, fair and foul. His corollary is, 'A square deal for everybody.' He does not ask his men to do anything that he himself will not do; if they keep the pace he is satisfied; he has no favorites."

Upon his retirement in 1915 (he had effectively stopped playing in 1911, making only 12 cameo playing appearances thereafter), Ernest J. Lanigan wrote, "Pittsburg is going to miss Clarke and so is the whole county. The only place that is to be congratulated is Winfield, Kansas."

CHAPTER 10

IT DID NOT TAKE LONG FOR BOSTON FANS TO BE REMINDED
THAT WISHIN', HOPING' AND TALKIN' DON'T WIN BASEBALL
GAMES. THE VISITING PIRATES SCORED FOUR RUNS OFF CY
YOUNG IN THE FIRST INNING AND THE HOME TEAM SPENT
THE REST OF THE DAY IN AN UNSUCCESSFUL CATCH-UP
POSTURE. THE FIRST GAME IN MODERN WORLD SERIES HIS-
TORY WENT TO PITTSBURG BY A 7-3 SCORE. IT WAS NOT A
HAPPY DAY AT THE HUNTINGTON AVENUE GROUNDS.

According to one account, when the game was over, "Into the highways
and byways the great concourse unwound itself. The spacious park gave
up that which it had absorbed, but it had exacted its tribute and the
laughter and gayety were gone. In place the throng walked out in
silence and pondered. The idols had been torn from their prior position, and the blow was hard to realize."

It had been a festive crowd, arriving early (shortly before noon) for the 3 p.m. start. According to the *Globe's* Melvin Webb, Jr., "By 2 o'clock and long before the first player on either team put in an appearance the first base bleachers and those behind third were packed solid with early comers, while each successive car coming up Huntington Ave. poured its human freight into the long lane leading to the ticket offices.

"A dozen extra policemen were pressed into service to keep the enthusiastic throng moving quickly through the turnstiles. Every seat in the grand stand was sold long beforehand, so that after 2 o'clock the crowd was turned loose into the field which was strongly roped off."

By the time the likes of Ferris, Chick Stahl, Dougherty and Criger came out for batting practice, so many people were crossing the field that it was impossible, Webb reported, for the players to "Hit 'em out."

When Cy Young made his presence known, the crowd erupted. "The appearance of (Young) brought every fan to his feet" because the veteran "was expected to pull off a victory for Boston today."

By 2:30 Webb estimated that more than 12,000 were in the stands.

Imagine the excitement level of a crowd in love with a sport and a team that they were convinced was the finest in the land.

"A crowd of 'Roxbury Rooters,'" wrote Webb, "every man of whom had an American flag, were the first to greet the Pittsburgs as they ran out onto the field for practice. The fast handling of the infield grounders sent out by Leever kept the crown cheering constantly. 'Kitty' Bransfield, an old Boston favorite and 'Hans' Wagner coming in for the lion's share of the applause. Phelps did the catching, and his throws down to second suggested that his arm is in fine trim to give

Criger a battle for the honors of nailing men at second."

Less than three hours later that happy crowd was morose.

What went wrong? What didn't? Start in the box, where the great master Cy Young was just an ordinary Joe.

The game began calmly enough. Beaumont flied to center and Clarke fouled to Criger. But the next six men reached base.

Leach started it all with a ground rule triple into the teeming right field crowd. He would have three more such blows before the Series concluded.

Wagner singled him home and then stole second. Bransfield reached safely on a Ferris error, with Wagner moving to third. Bransfeld stole second, and when Criger threw the ball away, Wagner scored. (Wasn't Criger going to control the Pittsburg running game?) Ritchey walked, and Clarke ordered a second successful double steal. Right fielder Jimmy Sebring singled home both men, making it 4-0. Phelps struck out, but the ball eluded Criger and now Ol' Cy needed to get his fifth out of the inning, which he got via a Philippe strike out.

The Pirates didn't need much more in the way of offense, but Sebring provided some insurance by knocking home a run with a third-inning single and by becoming the first man to hit a home run in modern World Series history when he hit one to center in the sixth inning and wound up touching 'em all, much to Tim Murnane's disgust.

Murnane's description: "Sebring hit a weak fly over Ferris that rolled nearly to the ropes, the Boston outfielders taking their time in fielding it and permitting a home run."

Not exactly Ruth calling his shot.

Infielder Tommy Leach of Pittsburg scored
the first run in World Series history.

The Boston battery came in for a little criticism. Everyone could live with Cy Young being a bit on the portly side in victory. But when things didn't go so well, those extra pounds were another matter. Hence: "Cy Young was looked on to win the money, but was not on edge. He looked several pounds too heavy."

As for poor Lou Criger, he was no longer the "prince of catchers" he had been a few hours before. Declared Murnane, "It was evident the visitors were going to force Criger to show his speed, and by so doing they made the Boston man look like a fur coat in July."

At the plate, the Boston batsmen didn't do much with Phillippe, the only quality Pittsburg pitcher not injured or battling mental illness. The Americans were down 7-0 in the seventh before they pushed across a pair of runs on back-to-back ground rule triples by Freeman and Parent and a LaChance sacrifice fly. A Wagner error, a Parent single and a second LaChance sacrifice fly produced a third run in the in ninth.

Thirty-one year-old Charles (Deacon) Phillippe, or Phillipi, as he was alternatively identified in the late stages of the series, had the odd distinction of being the only participant in the first World Series who had been born below the Mason-Dixon line. The general perception of turn-of-the-century baseball being dominated, or at least heavily populated, by southerners was at least a decade too soon, perhaps more. The truth was that the preponderance of the early ballplayers were from the north or the mid-west. But the Deacon had been born on May 23, 1872, in Rural Retreat, Virginia. He was one of the key players Dreyfuss had brought with him from Louisville, for whom he had made his debut in 1899. He established himself as an able pitcher who threw curve balls and liked to mind his own business. The word most frequently used in reference to him was "reticent."

A good case can be made that he was one of the most underrated pitchers in baseball history. A six-time 20-game winner, including each of his first five seasons, he retired at age 39 with a lifetime winning percentage of .639 (189-107). He spent his entire career playing for Barney Dreyfuss, that rare owner who prided himself on his loyalty and who had a policy of never selling players, only trading them for fellow human beings. Phillippe would last long enough to make a meaningful contribution to the 1909 World Champion Pirates, and he would go 14-2 as a utility pitcher on the 1910 Pirates.

The Deacon was on his game against the Americans in Game 1. He struck out 10, nailing every man in the Boston lineup except Buck Freeman. According to one account, Patsy Dougherty was particularly bothered by The Deacon's assortment of breaking balls, looking "completely at sea."

The Americans settled down after that rocky first inning, and, truth be told, had never really been outclassed. "The difference yesterday was in the pitcher's box," Murnane observed, "and it's not often that Uncle Cyrus fails to land the money, even if he is a bit fat."

One area where there was no apparent concern was the matter of umpiring, where Hank O'Day and Tommy Connolly were thoroughly professional. "Here was a pair of umpires who knew their business and the players never undertook to question their decisions," wrote Murnane, once again demonstrating that he was decades ahead of his time. Savvy scribes know that no sport can produce quality play absent quality officiating, and when it is particularly good it deserves mention in a game story.

The great crowd was a great source of journalistic fascination. It's not as if there hadn't been large crowds in attendance at Boston baseball games before. The *Globe* went out of its way to point out that there had been several larger gatherings during the regular season. But there was something different about this one, and it had to do with the enormity of the occasion. There had never been a twentieth century World Series game before. Everything taking place was history.

Observed Mel Webb, Jr.: "The fans might be classed as an inscrutable lot. At first thought one might be inclined to classify them among the narrow-minded, one-point-of-view people, but they are not. With all their hearts and lungs, they may wish that the team they bet on may skin the other side to the bone, but let a good, quick, exquisitely executed play be made by the visitors, and they will be found among the loudest of viciferators, and so it was yesterday. The "fans" like good ball, and it makes little difference whether it is the home team or the visiting team that puts it up, the applause of the "fan" is always forthcoming.

"From the first to the last inning there was no lull in the enthusiasm. Friends of the home team had seen more desperate games pulled away from the invaders and not for a moment did they lose hope. They contended that Collins' men had met a multitude of hard luck, and that they had not gotten into their stride.

"As the game progressed the home team did show better form, but the handicap of that awful first inning was too much for it, and many a Boston "fan" was disappointed when the game was over."

That's the way the Boston fans and media saw the Boston fans then, and a century later that's the way the Boston fans and media sees itself

Pittsburg pitcher Charles "Deacon" Phillippe recorded the first win in World Series history.

now. Boston takes a back seat to no municipality when it comes to propagating the idea that it is both baseball smart and extraordinarily magnanimous.

But it was not, in the end, a Boston day. It was a Pittsburg day. All in all, it had been a delightful afternoon for Pittsburg. Clarke was a sensation in left, roaming far and wide to snatch fly balls. Sebring had shown remarkable poise for a 21-year old. The baserunning had been exemplary. And The Deacon had been magnificent.

Manager Clarke's problem would be that he only had one Deacon Phillippe.

But that problem was not in evidence when the game ended. The Pirates and their joyous supporters went back to the Hotel Vendome, and sat down to training table and, we were told, "a general jollification." After that, the Pittsburg entourage headed to Keith's Theatre for a night of vaudeville.

The Boston fans sulked a bit and got their bets down on Big Bill Dinneen.

CHAPTER 11

IN FOOTBALL YOU MUST WAIT A WEEK TO ENACT REVENGE.
IN BASKETBALL AND HOCKEY IT'S TWO OR THREE
DAYS OR MORE.

But in baseball you bound out of bed a mere hours after a setback and get back to business.

That said, it took Big Bill Dinneen a mere hour and 47 minutes to put the smiles back on the faces of all the Boston backers.

Captain Collins' 21-game winner had the right stuff in Game 2, stifling the Pirates on three hits while striking out 11 as the Americans evened the series at one game apiece.

More history was made when Patsy Dougherty became the first man to hit two home runs in a single World Series game. The left fielder connected for a conventional inside-the-park job off starter and loser San Leever in the first, but it was home run number two, a sixth-inning blast off reliever Bucky Veil, that set tongues wagging.

For Dougherty's wallop landed on Huntington Avenue, and that had only happened once previously that season.

Tim Murnane was impressed. "His line drive over the left field fence was only the second time a ball was batted over the same fence, fair, and the performance will long be remembered by those present," he wrote. "The ball went like a shot close to the foul line, tipped the top of the fence and went over on to Huntington Ave."

It was further observed in the daily "Baseball Notes" that the last one was a peach. "He should tell the policemen to warn pedestrians along Huntington Ave."

Among the spectators witnessing Dinneen's domination of the Pirates was heavyweight great Gentleman Jim Corbett and team owner Henry Killilea, making a very rare in-person appearance at his own ballpark. The Milwaukee lawyer arrived in the morning, had, according to the *Globe* "a pleasant chat with the local players during the forenoon at the club's dressing room," and then left for home. He said he would see some of the games in Pittsburg.

Dinneen was given two runs to work with in the first inning, and he needed no more offensive aid. Dougherty got things started by hitting Leever's first pitch to deep right-center and then legging it around the bases. A Chick Stahl double and Freeman RBI single produced another run.

The big righty was in legitimate trouble just once. A leadoff walk to Beaumont, a Clarke single, and an infield out placed men on second and third with one out in the fourth inning. Wagner then lined one hard to Ferris, who was able to double Clarke off second for the inning-ending double play.

Dougherty supplied another helpful defensive play when he tossed out Claude Ritchey trying to stretch a leadoff single into a double in the eighth.

Wrote one literary admirer, "Claude is no slouch of a runner and gets over the ground in rapid style. Dougherty had to race to stop the ball and had to gather it cleanly and make an extraordinarily accurate throw. This is exactly what he did; it was a gem of a play."

Other than that, it was Dinneen and the Boston infield. There wasn't a single fly ball off the bat of a Pittsburg batter to the outfield until the seventh, when Leach flied to Stahl in center.

The infield play was sound on both sides, although the chap who authored the daily "Baseball Notes" was a bit more appreciative of the local quartet. So although "the work of (shortstop) Parent in the last two games has been simply grand," and "there was no playing for the grandstand, either," his appraisal of the Pirates' work was a bit harsher. "The Pittsburg infield works gracefully," he said, "but it is a shade too much 'grand stand,' to please the real old-timers, who like the get-there without the calcium light effects."

There was no doubt that this was a pitching-defense game. "Boston never slipped a cog, but was as steady as an ox on the field," said Murnane. "The visitors made a few misplays, but altogether proved to be a grand ball team."

Continued Murnane, "The fielding of the Boston men was a bit too speedy for the Dreyfuss crowd, which has had a season of easy mutton, and Dougherty rose to the occasion yesterday like a trout to fly in spring time."

The real concern for manager Clarke was the ineffective pitching of Leever, his number two pitcher. Clarke pulled his ailing right-hander from the game after one inning in favor of Veil, a former Bucknell ace who had only appeared in 12 games during the regular season. Veil pitched admirably, holding the Americans to just that Dougherty fence-clearer in the seventh. Strangely, he was never used in the Series again. He only was seen once the following season and that was the end of his major league career.

For the Boston fans, it simply seemed that the world had been placed back on its proper axis. This was the team they had been cheering for since April. Summarized Murnane, "The crowd pronounced the game one of the finest of the season, and the liberal applause given was proof that it was having a good time," he wrote. "Large sums of money changed hands, the Boston sports winning back what they had lost the day before and a little more."

More good news: Fred Clarke appeared to be desperate already. In Game 3 he'd be sending Deacon Phillippe to the mound on one-day's rest against a fresh 20-game winner, Long Tom Hughes.

Get those bets down, fellas.

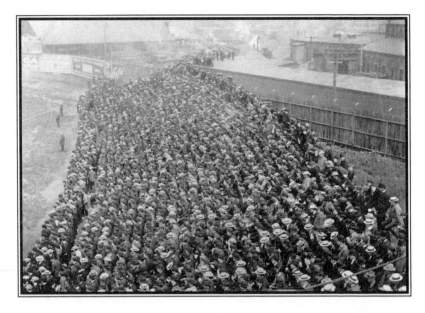

BOSTON'S CROWDS AT THE HUNTINGTON AVENUE GROUNDS
WELCOMED THE WORLD SERIES WITH GREAT ENTHUSIASM.

THE ROYAL ROOTERS (ABOVE) AND THE BOSTON BAND
(BELOW) KEPT SPIRITS HIGH AT ALL BOSTON HOME GAMES.

CHAPTER 12

ANY TIME SOME OLD-TIMER STARTS RHAPSODIZING ABOUT
THE SUPPOSED "GOOD OLD DAYS" IN AMERICAN SPORT,
GAME 3 OF THE 1903 WORLD SERIES CAN BE CITED AS
AN EXAMPLE THAT GREED AND A COMPLETE LACK OF
COMMON SENSE WAS AS MUCH A PART OF DOING
BUSINESS WAY-BACK-WHEN AS IT HAS BEEN AT ANY
TIME IN OUR EXISTENCE.

Almost undoubtedly, someone was going to lose Game 3 because of the absurd playing conditions. In some sort of perverse poetic justice, that team turned out to be the home team, the Boston Americans.

The words "crowd" and "control" did not appear to be linguistic partners to the management of the Boston team, as so many fans were allowed to penetrate the ballpark that, according to our friend Mr. Murnane, "the crowd pressed in upon the playing field and the outfielders were of little use."

The *Evening Globe* headlines pretty much tell the story.

SWARM ON THE FIELD

POLICE UNABLE TO CONTROL CROWD
AT BASEBALL GAME

ABOUT 30,000 THERE

VERY LIMITED SPACE FOR PLAY, THRONG
BEING CLOSE TO DIAMOND

How bad was it? The police resorted to rubber-hose swatting in order to subjugate the crowd. Boston business manager Joseph Smart was seen dispensing baseball bats to the constabularies as part of the crowd-control process. The entire affair would be unimaginable to a modern populace, but in those days owners had a very difficult time telling anyone who arrived at the park with money in his or her hand that admission to the grounds was not possible. The integrity of the game be damned.

Money, money, money . . . that's all the Boston ownership could think about. Said Mel Webb, "At 11 o'clock, four hours before the game began, a crowd of nearly 1,000 was clamoring for admission. With the opening of the gates at 12 o'clock there began a steady rush, which grew into a surging, struggling mass. The long lane leading to the ticket office was completely choked with the excited 'fans' and in the offices there was the merry ring of coins. With the ticket sellers it was simply a question of pulling in the money. The floors of the boxes were covered with specie, but the boys did not have a chance to pick it up.

"At 1:15 there was not a seat to be had in either of the bleachers and there was a fringe of black all around the ropes. These had been drawn nearly 75 feet nearer the diamond than yesterday or opening day."

At first, the crowd was festive. "There was a tooting of horns and a clamor of voices, mingled with the calls of the peanut and score-card boys," Webb reported. "In the bleachers there were frequent mix-ups, but everything seemed good-natured."

As gametime drew closer, however, the mood changed. "At 2:15 it was apparent that the police could not handle the crowd," said Webb. "A few men started away from the ropes in center field, then a thread of people strung out toward the end of the third-base bleachers, and next began a general stampede. Thousands broke over the ropes in one mad rush for the spaces in front of the third and first base bleachers. In vain the police tried to clear the field."

The players had difficulty preparing for the game. When the Pittsburg "Premiers," or "Pirates," came out, "it was impossible to bat any flies into the outfield, for no sooner had the team begun to work than there was another rush on the playing field, completely shutting in everything except the diamond itself."

Webb saluted efforts of one Boston policeman. He was "a big fellow, weighing nearly 300 pounds, but as agile as a kitten, who created no end of fun by his unique method of pushing back the crowd. He would throw his arms in the air and then run like a mad bull into the midst of the encroachers. His efforts had great effect, and when the other patrolmen followed his lead a large enough space was cleared to permit the game being started."

But it was all madness by our standards. At one point Pittsburg's Ginger Beaumont found it necessary to rescue two women who were in danger of being crushed by a major crowd movement. There more than likely never would have been a game at all had not 50 reserve officers not arrived to help control the crowd. They made good use of the rubber hose technique. "Their work was done according to the system and every moment saw the crowd pushed farther back," said Webb.

But how far back? It was agreed that baseballs hit into the crowd would be good for two bases, meaning there would definitely be some cheap hits. Meanwhile, so many fans had crowded between the fences along the first and third base lines and the wooden team benches provided for the players (dugouts were a future concept) that the teams were cut off from the customary seats and were forced to spend the entire afternoon sitting on the grass.

The first inning featured sparkling defensive plays by acknowledged masters Collins and Wagner. With two away and nobody on in the Pittsburg second, Boston's problems began. Claude Ritchey hit what should have been a routine fly ball toward left. It would have been a routine out number three on April 29, July 18, or September 21. But on October 3, with the ballpark holding more than double its capacity, it was a major annoyance for the Boston side.

Said Murnane, "Ritchey sent up a weak fly that Dougherty stood waiting for, only to see it drop into the crowd a few yards away, allowing the batsman two bases." Long Tom Hughes, not in his best form, walked Sebring. Phelps hit another soft fly, this one to center. But Chick Stahl "was standing close by to see the ball drop" as Ritchey scored.

Phillippe was on the mound for Pittsburg, and the Americans weren't able to do much. Well, there was a second inning shot hit by Candy LaChance that, according to Murnane, was "far over the crowd between center and left, a legitimate home run, but for the ground rules which held him at second." Hobe Ferris grounded out and the Americans couldn't score. So the home team was victimized both ways by its own crowd.

The third was another frustrating inning for the home team. Beaumont led off with a walk and Clarke hit yet another cheesy two-bagger into the crowd. When Leach singled home a run, Captain Collins decided it just wasn't going to be Long Tom's day and he summoned his icon, Young, who in the hours preceding the game had been seen sitting in the office helping the employees count the money. He had to move quickly from street clothes to his uniform when Collins first told him he'd be pitching.

Young was in excellent form, allowing just three hits and one eighth-inning unearned run (the key error being his own) in seven innings of work. The Americans reached Phillippe for single runs in the fourth and eighth, but he was in command, and when the 110 minutes of play was over he and the Pirates had themselves a 4-2 victory and a 2-1 World Series lead as the teams packed their belongings in anticipation of a trip to Pittsburg.

Murnane made it clear that the victor on this occasion was the team on whom the gods had smiled, not necessarily the team that had played a better game of baseball.

"There is no game in which luck plays so important a part as in baseball," he declared. "It seldom breaks even, but will follow one club for a while and then flirt with the next door neighbor, ready to change its abode at any moment. An even break is all that any club can look for, and all clubs look for this. The teams yesterday looked as evenly matched as two red hens pecking corn, and in a general manner it will be a clever man who can pick the winner.

"While the home team can have no real claim to a game where they only got in four safe hits, the fact remains that it was hard luck to lose on account of the crowd, for the four hits by Boston sent in two legitimate runs, while the winners scored only one run in the same manner."

Getting directly to the point, Tim Murnane said that "With a clear field the score would have been three to one in favor of Boston, thus showing that it was not a game in which Boston had been outplayed, although beaten."

One anonymous neutral print observer agreed completely. "It was the general verdict that the throng defeated the locals," he wrote. "There were not enough policemen to cope with the crowd and the result was that the outfielders could not field their positions and balls went for two-base hits that could easily have been outs under normal circumstances. Five balls were hit for the visitors that would have been easy outs with room for the outfielders to run....The great need of extra bleachers in their outfield, to which attention has been called again and again, was seen most decidedly."

The real story, of course, was baseball. In turn of the century

America it was the one and only team game of true universal consequence, with just about everything else tying for second place. Murnane tried to capture this phenomenon in his lead:

"Where is the genius who can explain the wonderful hold baseball has on the American public?" he inquired.

The people of Boston had been proving for more than 30 years that they loved the game, and now they had a chance to cheer for a great ball club against another great ball club, and on this Saturday afternoon, in this era of walk-up crowds, and with the home team tied in the Series, it was generally decided by the sports-loving populace of Boston that the Huntington Avenue Grounds was the place to be.

"It was no inhumane desire to see a bull fight or a bloody contest that drew the immense throng (announced as 18,801 but generally believed to be in excess of 25,000 and possibly as high as 30,000) to the American league park yesterday," said Murnane, "but a wholesome boyish desire to see the greatest ball teams on earth come together and battle for supremacy, with conditions so far as turf and weather as if made to order."

It was clear that the city of Boston was in love with the idea of a World Series to settle all bragging rights in the great game of baseball. Now it would be Pittsburg's turn. Said the author of the *Globe's* daily notes column known as "Echoes of the Game," "nearly 45,000 in three games is not bad. Now let us see how strong they are in Pittsburg."

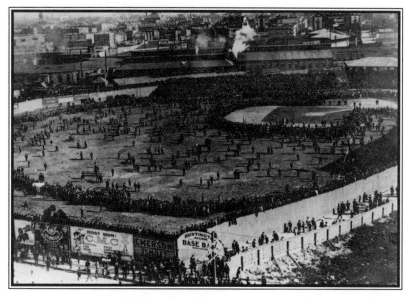

ABOVE: BECAUSE THERE WERE NO ATTENDANCE LIMITS AT
HUNTINGTON AVENUE GROUNDS, FANS OFTEN CROWDED THE
FIELD DURING THE GAMES.

BOX SCORE FROM GAME 3 AT HUNTINGTON AVENUE GROUNDS.
FINAL SCORE: PITTSBURG 4, BOSTON 2.

CHAPTER 13

Baseball fans never tire of arguing which players should and should not be in the Hall of Fame. Is it not time for members of SABR (Society for American Baseball Researchers) to take up the case for Barney Dreyfuss, the most neglected of all the great administrators and patrons in baseball history?

For nearly 40 years Barney Dreyfuss was one of the most influential figures in baseball. Surely, he was among the most intelligent men ever associated with a major league baseball club. Born on February 23,

1865 in Freyburg, Germany, he emigrated to these shores 17 years later to join a sister who was living in Paducah, Kentucky.

Small (5-feet-4) and not exactly robust, he began working in the Bernheim Distillery Company. He started out scrubbing down whiskey barrels for $8 a week, but his superiors quickly learned that the German fellow had a genius for numbers, and soon he was doing their books. After one month he was promoted to credit manager.

Doctors told him he needed to get outdoors more for health, and since he had already demonstrated an interest in this American sport known as baseball, he was given a job with the company baseball team, this being, of course, an era when every company imaginable had its own team. His sister was married to a Bernheim who was friendly with men who ran the Louisville team of the National League, and Barney was soon dispatched to Louisville to run the business operation of the club. It did not take long for Barney Dreyfuss to go from interested stockholder and super bookkeeper to team president—he bought out his partners for $50,000 in 1899.

The National League was undergoing a shakedown period. After the collapse of both the American Association and the Players League, the National League stumbled through the '90s as a 12-team league whose style of play was borderline barbaric. At the conclusion of the 1899 season, the league decided to drop four franchises, one of which was Louisville.

The team was loaded with talent, and Dreyfuss took 14 of his Louisville players when the team merged with the Pittsburg club and moved all the players to the Smoky City for the 1900 season. Among the players he brought with him to Pittsburg were future Hall of

Famers Honus Wagner, Fred Clarke and Rube Waddell.

The team was the first great club of the twentieth century. Pittsburg finished second to Brooklyn in 1900, but the "Premiers," as they were sometimes known, won the 1901 pennant by 7-1/2 games over Philadelphia; won the 1902 pennant by 27-1/2 games over Brooklyn, a record margin that has now lasted more than a century; and, despite losing some key players in the face of the National League-American League war, won the 1903 pennant by 6-1/2 games over New York.

Dreyfuss was respected for actually knowing something about the game, and when it came to business practices, he was looked up to by everyone. A close friend of National League president Harry Pulliam, he was a central figure in the battle between the leagues, first, by clever maneuverings that protected his Pittsburg territory against American League encroachment, and then, when the bloodletting was getting too severe, by helping to broker a lasting peace between the leagues.

He ran a unique shop. According to one Chester L. Smith in the *Pittsburg Press*, Dreyfuss "never sold a player for the cash he could get out of the deal." He was simply put off by the notion of a ballplayer being a piece of property.

So it was hardly surprising that two decades later he would register public disapproval over the systematic dismantling of the Boston Red Sox by owner Harry Frazee, who created the Yankee dynasty we know today by peddling players to New York for what we would refer to in these times as the "Benjamins."

Again from Chester Smith: "He (Dreyfuss) was caustic in his denunciation of the succession of trades and purchases which sent a greater part of the Boston Red Sox to the New York Yankees, a move which deliberately wrecked the former club and made the latter a perennial contender."

It was Barney Dreyfuss' custom to invest money for any player who wished him to do so, and to make it a money-back guarantee. "While he would not guarantee what return might be expected," said Mr. Smith," he promised there would be no loss."

Among his other services, Barney Dreyfuss, like the NBA's legendary owner-coach Eddie (The Mogul) Gottlieb four decades down the road, made up the playing schedule. When he died in 1932, an anonymous obituary writer declared that "all other magnates relied on the experienced veteran to straighten out the schedule, and conflicts in dates, hard railroad jumps and unequal distribution of holiday home games. Where the other magnates had to ponder, Barney had it all at the ends of his fingers."

Always thinking ahead, he owned one of the first automobiles in Pittsburg.

He was the man whose personal challenge to Boston owner Henry Killilea had made possible the 1903 World Series, and now he was excited about playing host to the American League visitors for Games 4, 5, 6 and 7. But he would have been even more excited if he had been able to put on the games in a more suitable venue.

The Pittsburg National League franchise had been playing its games in Exposition Park since 1891. The Allegheny Tradesmen's Industrial Institute had been the original occupant of the site, located on the Allegheny River, near the covered bridge between Pittsburg's Exposition Buildings and the lower part of Allegheny City. When the building burned down, the edifice was razed and the site was given over to entertainment interests—and, yes, that was plural.

For there was more than just baseball taking place at Exposition Park. Baseball had to share the spot with bike racing (an enormously popular activity at the time), not to mention circuses and large tent shows of all kinds.

The big problem with Exposition Park, however, was water. Its location at the juncture of the Allegheny and Monongahela Rivers just about guaranteed flooding would take place. The granddaddy of 'em all took place on July 4, 1902, when 10,000 fans showed up for the morning half of a doubleheader and found a foot and a half of water in the outfield. There had been such heavy rain that the sewers had backed up. Nowadays, it would be a rain check and see you tomorrow, or whenever. But impresarios were not so easily defeated in those days. People wanted to see a ballgame or two, and they had money jingling in their pockets. Amazingly, baseball life went on. The teams agreed that anything hit into the outfield was a ground-rule *single.*

Things got worse in the afternoon, because the waters, still in the process of rising, came within 20 feet of second base. Newspaper wags nicknamed the place "Lake Dreyfuss," but the games were played, and the Pirates/Premiers took two.

It was a problem that would never go away. In 1908, one year before Dreyfuss opened the futuristic Forbes Field, he purchased baseball's first tarpaulin for $2000. It was made of brown paraffin duck and attached to a truck 10 x 15 feet and 3 feet high.

Barney Dreyfuss solved his water problems, and many other irritations, with Forbes Field. His team won the 1909 World Series and he remained in charge of the Pirates until his death 23 years later. When he died, journalists went into overdrive praising a gentleman who enjoyed universal respect in the game.

"He was a good fighter," said John Kieran of the *New York Times*, "but he was also clear-headed enough to know when and how to offer a peace treaty."

When he died, he was the last of the principals from the American League-National League turn-of-the-century war to do so. He had been the reigning institutional memory of baseball's key historical moment.

Pittsburg writer Ralph S. Davis said, "The Last of the Mohicans— that's Barney Dreyfuss, sole active survivor of an era when baseball spikes had long, sharp blades and when men invested their money in the National Game because they loved it as a sport rather than regarded it as a business. These were men who were fan-magnates who thought more of a victory by their team than they did a dividend from their club."

In 1932 baseball celebrated another successful World Series amid a predictable amount of reflection and self-congratulation. But an anonymous observer, reading and listening and reading and listening without coming across a certain name, exploded in print, "It would verge on the border of criminal neglect if the great Barney Dreyfuss would be forgotten, as he seems to have been, in the wake of the most recent and lucrative World Series. Every aspect of the colorful classic was covered in minute detail and in a most competent and cogent manner with the mammoth exception of Barney's contribution. He not only originated it in 1903 against the vile vituperation of the game's powerful reactionaries.

"As a schedule maker, Mr. Dreyfuss had no peer. Since his death the schedules have provided great controversy, and, at times were ludicrous. So a few lines of respectful tribute would not be amiss, particularly at World Series time. It was his brain child."

In 1953, when baseball celebrated the Golden Anniversary of its most important activity, New York writing legend Dan Daniel found himself thinking of the World Series creator. "There is no effigy of Barney Dreyfuss. There is no memorial to the vision, acumen and vital contribution to the game of the one-time owner of the Pittsburgh Pirates."

If he had done nothing else, Barney Dreyfuss would be remembered for a singular act of generosity. The Boston Americans, you may recall, were livid about the financial split of the proceeds offered them by owner Henry Killilea. Barney Dreyfuss faced no such mutiny. He announced that he would donate the management take to the players' pool. The 1903 Pittsburg Pirates have remained the only team in baseball history to receive more money in losing a World Series than their opponents did in winning it.

"As usual," reminded John Kieran, "he emerged in the mantle of the victorious martyr. Always remember he contributed the entire proceeds for division among his team. No other owner has ever since duplicated this generous gesture."

That was written more than 70 years ago. The meter is still running.

Top and bottom: The World Series moved to an equally Electric Exposition Park in Pittsburg for Games 4 through 7.

CHAPTER 14

THE BOSTON AMERICANS WOULD NOT BE GOING TO
PITTSBURG ALONE. THE "ROYAL ROOTERS," 125 STRONG,
WERE ALSO ON THE TRIP.

Always welcome, the Rooters would prove to have more of an effect on the Series than any group of "cranks," or "fans," had ever had before. But even they had no idea what was going to happen before they left Pittsburg.

Captain Collins and his boys were predictably confident as they boarded the 10:45 a.m. train to the Smoky City. "The train bearing the team and the rooters goes through Albany and Buffalo and is due to arrive in the land of "perpetual smoke" at 6:30 this morning," reported the morning *Globe*.

Collins' mound choice to tie the Series was Big Bill Dinneen. Fred Clarke, with fewer viable options, would have to send Deacon Phillippe out there for the third time in four games.

That being the case, no one in Pittsburg was too unhappy when rain forced postponement of Game 4.

Pitching on two days rest, Phillippe was again masterful for eight innings. He took a comfortable 5-1 lead into the ninth, but the Americans threw a big scare into him, scoring three times and leaving two men on when pinch-hitter John O'Brien popped to second, leaving Pittsburg with a shaky 5-4 victory (and a 3-1 Series lead).

It had been a 2-1 game entering the seventh. The big blow was a two-run triple by Tommy Leach, one of the innumerable three-baggers put in the books during the Pittsburg portion of the Series. Once again, people were permitted on the actual playing field; hence, the need for daily ground rules.

Murnane's partisanship was obvious. The great scribe had seen the Boston boys play too much good baseball during the regular season for him to believe it could be losing to Pittsburg legitimately.

"The game today was very much like the first and third games of the series," he said, "where Pittsburg had the luck and was always quick to take advantage of openings, while Boston appeared reluctant to out up the raise, fearing a second raise, and not caring to go through.

"The batting rally of the Boston men in the ninth was as refreshing to the Boston rooters as a breath of east wind on a warm day, and the only out about it was that it didn't last long enough. It had the effect, however, of showing Pittsburg that nothing but a continual hustle to the end will win games from Boston. With Cyrus Young in tomorrow, the trouble will continue, for the Collins tribe are gritty."

The big news took place off the field, where the Royal Rooters, accompanied by a musical aggregation known as the Guenther Band, made themselves known. The Rooters and the band marched into Exhibition Park together some 25 minutes before the start of the game, with many of the Rooters dashing inside to be sure they could serve as a welcoming committee for the Boston players, who were part of the parade procession.

"The parade of the rooters through the streets was the principal talk of the Pittsburg people," wrote one local anonymous scribe. "The band was given seats in the first two rows of Section J, which was behind the Boston bench, and their selections during the afternoon were very enjoyable."

Captain Collins was not having such a good time. His team was trailing in the Series, three games to one, and they were down to a one-man pitching staff.

But Capt. Collins had to be feeling good about Game 5. He had Uncle Cyrus ready to go.

For once the Americans would not have to look at Deacon Phillippe. Fred Clarke had little choice but to entrust this throwaway game to William F. (Brickyard) Kennedy, a colorful 35-year-old right-hander who had gone 9-6 during the regular season. No one expected a great deal from him, and so no one was surprised when Boston blasted him for 11 hits and 10 runs (only four earned) in seven innings of work in what would turn out to be the final appearance of a 12-year major league career.

It was actually a legitimate pitcher's duel for five innings. The Americans benefited from some shaky Pittsburg defense in the sixth—even the impeccable Wagner threw one to an uncovered base—and played a lot of what we would today label as "small ball," before Young, a .300 hitter during the regular season, took advantage of the crowd situation to lace a ground-rule triple that brought home LaChance and Ferris. Pat Dougherty followed with a more legitimate triple to left, bringing home Young with the sixth run of the inning. The Americans went on to win, 11-2, narrowing the Series lead to 3-2.

LIKE ITS BOSTON COUNTERPART, EXPOSITION PARK TURNED
NO FAN AWAY, RESULTING IN A PLAYING FIELD THAT WAS SOMETIMES
OVERRUN WITH SPECTATORS.

Royal Rooter with flag

Game 5 proved to be the Series turning point in more ways than one. For Game 5 was the birth of "Tessie" as a tactical weapon.

"Tessie" was a popular song of the day. "Tessie" was a hit song from a production entitled "The Silver Slipper," and was popularized first by W.S. Hawkins and later Joseph Welch. It had nothing to do with baseball. Then again, what do "YMCA" or "Na-Na-Hey-Hey, Kiss Him Goodbye" have to do with baseball? When sports and music intersect, logic is often a victim.

For some reason, Nuf Ced McGreevey and the rest of the Royal Rooters decided to start singing "Tessie" during Game 5. The Rooters liked it and the Boston players liked it. The Pittsburg fans and the Pittsburg players did not like it, and they let it irritate them. Suddenly, "Tessie" was Capt. Collins' 10th man.

"I think those Boston fans actually won that Series for the Red Sox," Tommy Leach would say decades later in Lawrence Ritter's magnificent baseball tale, *The Glory of Their Times.* "We beat them three out of the first four games, and then they started singing that damn 'Tessie' song, their Red Sox fans did. They called themselves the Royal Rooters, and their leader was some character named Mike McGreevey, because any time there was an argument about anything to do with baseball he was the ultimate authority. McGreevey gave his opinion that ended the argument: nuf sed!

"Anyway," Leach continued, "in the fifth game of that Series the Royal Rooters started singing 'Tessie' for no particular reason at all, and the Red Sox won. They must have figured it was a good-luck charm, because from then on you could hardly play ball they were singing 'Tessie' so loud."

THE LYRICS:

"Tessie is a maiden with a sparkling eye,
Tessie is a maiden with a laugh;
Tessie doesn't know the meaning of a sigh,
Tessie's lots of fun and full of chaff.
But sometimes we have a little quarrel, we two
Tessie always turns her head away
Then it's up to me to do as all boys do,
So I take her hand to mine and say

(Chorus)

Tessie, you make me feel so sadly,
Why don't you turn around?
Tessie, you know I love you madly;
Babe, my heart weighs about a pound.
Don't blame me if I ever doubt you,
Tessie, you are the only, only, only.

Tessie has a parrot that she loves quite well,

Polly's just learning how to woo;
Tessie tells him everything she has to tell,
Polly thinks he knows a thing or two.
Tessie gave a party at her home one night,
Polly said he'd like to sing a song;

Tessie never thought she'd seen a bird so bright,
When Polly started off in accents strong."

(Chorus)

The Rooters were devilish improvisers. They went after poor old Brickyard Kennedy, in his own ballpark, singing:

"Kennedy, you seem to pitch so badly
Take a back seat and sit down.
Kennedy, you are a dead one
And you ought to leave the town.
Pittsburg needs a few good pitchers,
such as Boston's pennant lifters.
Phillipi, you are the only, only, only one."

Consider that Pittsburg drew almost 13,000 people for that game, and a mere 125 of them, give or take a bowler hat, were members of the Royal Rooters. How could so few be so disruptive, and so annoying, to so many?

They just were. "Sort of got on your nerves after a while," said Leach. "And before we knew what happened; we'd lost the World Series."

The Rooters made the newspapers for another reason. The Guenther band that had been their musical accompaniment for Game 4 was suing Nuf Ced and his Royal Rooters compatriot Charles Lavis for breach of contract, claiming that the Bostonians had hired them to play for four days but had let them go after the first day in order to hire another band and now refused to pay for the remaining three days.

Lavis contended that the band had only been hired for one day since the Rooters didn't have enough money to spring for four days of music, and wouldn't be hiring another band until the Boston team won a game and the Rooters could collect on their side bets. "I did not hire the Greater Pittsburg (i.e. Guenther) Band for four days," Lavis insisted. "I hired it for one day."

Lavis said he was gratified with the support he had received from Pittsburg fans in the matter. "I desire to thank the good people of Pittsburg for their generous offers of assistance," he said. "We are surely not without friends in an enemy's country."

CHAPTER 15

IN THE EYES OF EVERYONE CONNECTED WITH
BOSTON, THE AMERICANS LED THE SERIES, TWO GAMES
TO THREE. IT WAS OVER ALREADY, EVEN IF THE
PITTSBURG FANS DIDN'T KNOW IT.

The issue was simple. This wasn't some turn-of-the-century version of T-ball. This was hard ball, big-league style, and what is true today was equally as true a century ago: pitching dominates. And poor Fred Clarke had plumb run out of quality pitchers for Game 6.

The Deacon had already answered the bell magnificently, winning three times in the first four games. How much could he have left? And who else did Clarke have? Sam Leever's arm was aching from the minute he got done till the time he finally fell asleep. Brickyard was finished. There was that kid, Veil, but just because he had fooled the Americans once doesn't mean he could do it again. Clarke really could have used Big Ed Doheny, but that poor guy had problems a lot more severe than trying to figure out how to win a World Series game.

On the other side, Big Bill Dinneen and Cy Young were ready to go, as was a third 20-game winner, Long Tom Hughes. It was an unfortunate pitching mismatch, but that was surely the way it was.

With the weather a bit overcast, the desperate Pittsburg management was pushing for a postponement of Game 6, but Collins wasn't buying it. He knew Clarke was just trying to find a way to help Phillippe, but that was too bad. There was no reason not to play Game 6, as scheduled.

The Boston players had picked up the victory scent.

"The people of Boston can rest assured that Boston will win the series," said Charles Farrell, the Duke of Marlboro. "We have Pittsburg on the run. They have but one good pitcher, and though Phillippi (everyone, including headline writers, used 'Phillippe' and 'Phillippi' interchangeably) has beaten us three times, he cannot do it twice more, unless he is a wonder of wonders. I do not think either Veil or (J.D.) Thompson can do anything to us now that we have started batting, and it will be up to Phil to do the trick twice.

"It will give me a great deal of satisfaction to win after we got off to such a bad start," continued the Duke. "There are people back in Boston who quit easily when we lost the first game in Boston; a lot of them said we might as well quit."

But quitting never entered the Americans' minds. Not after Game 1; not after Game 4; and certainly not after Game 6.

BILL DINNEEN HAS THE GOODS

BIG CROWD TRIES TO RATTLE HIM

GETS SUPPORT FROM ROYAL ROOTERS

Those were the morning headlines over Boston's series leveling 6-3 triumph in Game 6. Now the Series was turned on its ear.

"It was a glorious victory," trumpeted Tim Murnane, "won by superior all-around ballplaying, and in the face of whirlwind rooting for the home team."

The Royal Rooters had touched a nerve. The Pittsburgs couldn't allow 200 boisterous Bostonians (reinforcements had arrived) to out-cheer them, could they?

They cheered. They sang. And they threw paper. "In an attempt to disconcert the visiting team," said Murnane, "baskets of fine paper were flung to the breeze and hung in the air and covered the field." Paper landed on Dinneen, but he remained impervious, pitching the strong game Capt. Collins needed for his team to knot the Series.

Leever pitched well, sore arm and all, but he was let down by a shoddy Pittsburg defense, as throwing errors by both Leach at third and Wagner at short (not having the Series everyone anticipated) accounted for four of Boston's six runs. There were 12,000 people jammed into Barney Dreyfuss's stadium, and so, naturally, that meant many of them had taken up residence on the playing field, and thus there were triples by Chick Stahl and Freddy Parent.

What made the biggest impression on observers from both sides was

Boston's defense. It was now generally acknowledged that the infield in particular might be the finest the sport, now in its seventh decade, had ever seen.

Pat Egan, acknowledged by Murnane as the "clever baseball critic" of the *Pittsburg Times,* had this to say: "Boston's infield worked like a clock yesterday, and everybody on it took some part in one or more hair-raising stops or plays. Collins demonstrated that he is as fast as ever when he jumped with the agility of a cat for a short bunt down along the third-base line and threw out the runner by a block at first. The clever manner in which he executed his plays served notice on the Pirates that they would have to take desperate chances if they bunted the ball in the neighborhood of the Boston captain. LaChance showed too much better advantage, while Parent made it clear enough to the crowd that Wagner has nothing to speak of on him. No infield ever worked better, and several of the chances were extremely difficult to handle."

Murnane was in agreement, as one might suspect. "The features of the fielding were one fast play by LaChance to Parent at second for a force out and a return of the ball at first for what looked like a sure out," Murnane said. "Collins killed two bunts by running one-hand pick-ups and sharp throws. Ferris made two fine running assists. The work of Parent was superb and made the great Wagner look cheap."

Parent, who knew the entire baseball world felt that shortstop would be a mismatch in the Series, was starting to feel pretty good about everything. "Boston will win," he said. "These fellows stop when you once get a lead on them and they have nothing on us at any time."

Murnane was a full believer in the cause. "Baseball is the sole topic of conversation in this city tonight," he wrote. "The two victories of Boston over the Pittsburg champions have convinced people that Boston has a better ball club than the people here were led to believe. This is, of course, a National League City, with very little knowledge of the strength of the American League.

"The crowing of the National League people, like Pres. Pulliam, Jim Hart of Chicago, John McGraw and others, to the effect that Pittsburg would eat up the Boston men had the effect of giving the local followers of the game false confidence. Now the illusion is dispelled and they realize Pittsburg must return to Boston for the longest proposition of a lifetime."

CHAPTER 16

ON OCTOBER 9, 1903, JIMMY COLLINS RECEIVED A
TELEGRAM AT HIS PITTSBURG HOTEL....

TO JAMES J. COLLINS,
MANAGER AND CAPTAIN OF THE
BOSTON BASEBALL TEAM, PITTSBURG, PENN:

The Boston Globe, believing that victory is
within the grasp of you and your comrades,
offers to present to each player of the Boston
team of the American League, if it brings to
Boston the world's championship, a valuable
gold medal, which can be worn as a watch
charm, and be treasured as a reminder of the
most notable achievement upon the diamond.

CHAS. H. TAYLOR, EDITOR

Underneath the text of the telegram, the *Globe* offered additional explanation:

"Never before have the leaders of two great leagues battled for supremacy in the national sport. The public interest in the final result is therefore unusual.

"The Boston Globe shares in the general desire of New Englanders that Capt. Collins and his men, who have made such a fine and somewhat uphill fight in the series with the Pittsburg players, should bring the World's Championship in triumph to Boston. It belongs here, for this long has been the best ball town in the country. The prize should be ours, for ours is the highest talent this year that the diamond has seen.

"Beautiful gold medals, one for each of the Boston players if the series is won by Boston for Boston, are offered by the Globe as an added incentive to strenuous endeavor. Those medals will be worth the gaining because of their beauty, but they will be most prized by their possessors in the years to come as souvenirs of the most famous series of baseball games ever played."

The story would take on a predictable life of its own, especially inside the pages of the *Boston Globe,* which was now actively selling the idea that winning the medals was the incentive the Boston team needed to boost itself over the top in the grand struggle with the boys from Pittsburg.

First, of course, there was the requisite thank-you from Capt. Collins, printed in you-can't-miss-it bold type:

> I fully appreciate the sentiment expressed in your telegram. It is simply following out a policy that has made the Globe a great factor in the national game. It is pleasing to get such recognition, and such loyal and liberal support. The boys will do everything in their power to win the honor for Boston, which has given us the best treatment, even when we were not having the best luck.
>
> JAMES J. COLLINS, Captain Boston Americans

And how could Fred Clarke not play the proper gentleman and add his own comments?

> It looks well to see the press recognize the game and the players in this way. The Boston Globe has, for years, been recognized as the authority on the game, and the Boston boys are to be congratulated upon having such a supporter, but Pittsburg intends to take this series and prevent any handing over of the Globe's gold medals.
>
> FRED CLARKE, Captain Pittsburg Nationals

On the morning of Game 7, the *Globe* could not resist patting itself on the back. "Whenever in Boston men gathered last evening, whether in hotels, in theatres, clubs, bowling alleys, billiard rooms or street corners, the general topic of conversation was baseball—the championship series between the Boston Americans and the Pittsburg Nationals; the closeness of the series and the gold medals which have been offered to the Boston players by the Globe," wrote someone, quite possible loyal Globie Tim Murnane.

"The excitement is more widely spread and more intense over this contest between the champions of both the great league than was ever known before in the history of baseball in this city. The offer of the Globe to present each member with a valuable gold medal if the team brings to Boston the world's championship has intensified the local interest, if such a thing were possible in the present context."

Truly desperate now, Fred Clarke did what any man in his position would have done. He played the weather card, declaring that Game 7 would have to wait another day due to inclement weather.

It wasn't rain, but wind and cold that made it impossible to play, he said.

Collins was livid. "What's the matter with you people?" he demanded.

"Nothing," replied Clarke. "But it's too cold to play today."

Fred Clarke needed another day for Deacon Phillippe; that's all there was to it. Jimmy Collins would have followed the same path, were he in Clarke's shoes.

There was one other consideration. Pushing the game back from a Friday to a Saturday enabled Barney Dreyfuss to take advantage of a Westinghouse offer to purchase 1,000 tickets the giant firm would not have purchased on a weekday.

A gigantic crowd of 17,038 poured into Exposition Park, so once again there was a guarantee of ground-rule triples by somebody. Win or lose, this was going to be the last day of baseball in Pittsburg for the 1903 season, so the fans had come ready to make some noise.

CHAPTER 17

THE BOSTON PLAYERS NOW HAD THE EXTRA INCENTIVE OF
THE GOLD MEDALS BEING OFFERED BY THE GLOBE'S
CHARLES TAYLOR. PITTSBURG OWNER BARNEY DREYFUSS
RESPONDED IN THE FINEST AMERICAN WAY, BY DANGLING
DOLLAR BILLS IN FRONT OF HIS OWN PLAYERS' EYES.

"If the Pittsburg team beats Boston in the championship series now on they will receive every cent of money coming to Pittsburg less expenses incurred," Dreyfuss announced on the eve of Game 7.

The translation was that he would take no money from the Series for himself or his franchise, per se. Every cent of the Pittsburg profits would go to the players. The estimate of the bounty was $25,000. It was later revealed that the generous Pittsburg owner had made the offer to Fred Clarke back on September 28 before it was definitely settled that the series would be played.

Back in Boston, things were far from tranquil, as the morning paper revealed.

TROUBLE OVER TICKETS

COMPLAINTS ABOUT SPECULATORS CORNERING THE SUPPLY, AND PATRONS ARE INDIGNANT

The Americans, of course, said they had no idea how anything could have gone amiss. According to Mr. H.A. McBreen, the assistant manager, the box office was opened in the morning in order to sell tickets for Games 8 and 9, but it was closed as soon as "substantial evidence was reported that speculators were practicing their cunning to get hold of large blocks."

Well, that's exactly what was going on, and vox populi was incensed. According to the *Globe,* "Several exceedingly vexed men who delight in a good game of ball were so hot under the collar when they called at the Globe office to complain that only the speculators had seats to sell that the rain of the forenoon hissed when it ran down their backs."

Angry baseball fans were complaining that tickets by the hundreds were in the hands of speculators who "hawked their 'cornered' goods in front of the shops where patrons of the game should get their cards of admission for the laying down of a single 'punk.'"

The *Globe,* which a year hence would actually own the team, went into a 1903 version of damage control on behalf of the beleaguered club officials.

"The same at the ground was closed down early," the Globe report-ed, "for the reason that orders from all over New England had arrived by telegraph. First orders, of course, received first attention. A goodly number of tickets had to be reserved for the players, who buy for their friends. There are no free tickets."

There still aren't. A century later, all playoff tickets are paid for by someone. And a century later, there are still moans and groans at every big sporting and entertainment event that gobs of tickets fall into the nefarious hands of ticket speculators, or as we call them today, "scalpers." No one ever knows how they get them. It is one of American life's eternal mysteries, right there with how a man's socks are somehow gobbled up by his wife's washing machine.

However the good people of Pittsburg obtained their tickets, a record number of them packed Exposition Park hoping that the noble Deacon Phillippe had one more victory stored in his trusty right arm. But though he pitched fairly well, the strain of a fourth start in 10 days was evident as the Americans reached him for 11 hits, bunching enough of them to come away with a 7-3 victory and a 4-3 lead in the series.

Such an overflow crowd meant there would be bogus extra base hits, and this time the Fates turned on Pittsburg, as it was the Boston squad that benefited most handsomely from the necessary ground rules. The Americans smacked five triples, two of which, by Capt. Collins and Chick Stahl, came during a two-run first inning.

The rain had stopped, it had warmed up some and the wind had shifted, but the field was in predictably poor condition and the whole affair looked more as if there should have been an English soccer match taking place than a baseball game.

"The scene was a weird one," declared Murnane. "Clouds of black smoke from the large steel works came sailing down the two rivers than meet here from the Ohio, while a bright sun shot heedless through the whirling sheets of light and heavy smoke, and every face was focused on the home plate as Boston's curly-haired boy and his favorite club stood ready for business."

The beauty of a game that featured seven errors was clearly in the eye of the beholder. Whereas an envoy from the *Pittsburg Post* declared the game to be "sad, chilly and tedious," and the Pittsburg papers, when not (legitimately) bemoaning Phillippe's worn-out state, made reference to exhausted players slipping all over a slick surface, Murnane saw only elegance, beauty and Boston dominance.

"The last play of the day by Ferris and Parent was worth a trip to Pittsburg to see," he gushed. "The young men to shine with the greatest brilliancy during the day were Collins, Ferris, Criger, Young, Stahl and Freeman, with Uncle Cyrus the brightest star of all.

"For Pittsburg Bransfield, Phelps, Ritchey and Clarke did some extra fine work. The umpiring of Tom Connolly and Hank O'Day was simply great. Tonight the series stands four to three in Boston's favor, and Boston people will have a chance to see the finish of a wonderful series."

Ol' Uncle Cyrus was touched for 10 hits, but they were too scattered to do enough damage.

Typical of the afternoon's game flow was the seventh. With one out Young walked Phelps. "The crowd set up a din to rattle the Boston pitcher," Murnane reported, "but the old boy refused to quit, and fanned Phillipe and forced Beaumont to raise one out to Dougherty. Then came 'Tessie, my darling, how I love you,' and a rousing three times three from the Boston contingent."

By now the game had almost become secondary to the rousing Battle of the Bands.

The whole "Tessie" business had embarrassed Pittsburg into action. By now Pittsburg had produced its own band, and its first official action early in the day was to make an attempt to drown out a Boston rendition of "Tessie" by playing "Yankee Doodle" concurrently.

Among the musical selections played by one band or another were "America," "Wearing of the Green," "Dixie, "Annie Laurie" and "My Maryland."

The Pittsburg fans surely had given their all. There had been a procession of some 500, armed with horns and megaphones, that had made its way to the park, and included among the marchers were some prominent Pittsburg businessmen. It was reported that trains had disgorged people from Wheeling, Steubenville, Uniontown, Connellsville, Blairsville, Indian, Charleroi, Beaver Falls and Monangahela City, among other locales.

"The home players came out to the field at 1:45, and they were received with a roar of applause," Murnane said. "The crowd seemed fairly wild and cheered every move of the local players. At 2:10, when the Boston players pushed their way through the spectators, they were greeted with a combination of cheers and hoots."

There just wasn't anything Captain Clarke, Dreyfuss, or any of those rabid fans could do about the fact that the Pittsburg team only had one pitcher to count on, and he was wearing out. Said one neutral observer, "It is too bad that the Pittsburg club should be so sorely handicapped in the pitching department. With Leever and Doheny in shape, there is no doubt they could have made a better showing than has been the case. President Dreyfuss was advised not to play the series with the team in a crippled condition, but he insisted upon doing so."

Frank B. McQuiston of the *Pittsburg Dispatch* put it this way on the morning of Game 7: "The Pittsburg club did not win the championship of the National league with one pitcher, nor had they the right to defend it with but one.…It would not have been an act of cowardice for the owners of the Pittsburg club to announce plainly that, owing in the falling of Doheny and the bad cold in the shoulder of Sammy Leever, they did not feel able to fight against the American league club.

"Should the American league be the loser," he continued, "people will be sore indeed, and will have reason to be, because they will have been beaten by a one-man team. Phillippi will, if he wins, be the most famous player in the history of baseball. He will be famous even if he loses out now, for he alone has been the man."

The Sunday *Pittsburg Post* had run a photograph of Phillippe with a caption saying that "he went to the rubber too often." The fans appreciated the great effort Phillippe was putting forth, so much so that when he came to bat against Cy Young in the third inning, a man named Barney Arena, representing a group of Pittsburg followers, came to the plate to present Phillippe with a diamond stickpin. The crowd applauded tremendously, and Phillippe showed his gratitude by lashing a single to left.

Back on the gold-medal front, Captain Collins had responded to Charles Taylor by telegram on behalf of the team.

EXPOSITION PARK,
PITTSBURG, OCT. 10
GEN. CHAS. H. TAYLOR, THE BOSTON GLOBE

On behalf of the Boston players I thank you
for your liberal offer. I assure you the boys appreciate your kindness, coming as it does from one
who has always been a friend of the national
game.

JAMES COLLINS, CAPTAIN OF THE BOSTON AMERICANS

And the players got into the act, as well:

PITTSBURG, PENN., OCT. 10
TO GEN. C.H. TAYLOR, EDITOR OF THE BOSTON GLOBE:

We, the undersigned members of the Boston
American baseball club, thank you for your
graceful compliment and tender of medals. Win
or lose, we appreciate your courtesy and remem-
brance.

SIGNED: CAPT. COLLINS, YOUNG, CRIGER,
DOUGHERTY, FREEMAN, GIBSON, HUGHES, LACHANCE,
PARENT, FERRIS, C. STAYHL, J. STAHL, FARRELL,
O'BRIEN, DINNEEN, WINTER

The *Globe* printed a design for the medals, which, the readers were
assured, "represent the reversion from the type of huge, shapeless mass-
es of metal which were popular a few years ago. These are almost tiny,

being designed to hang as an ornament to a watch chain, but their meaning is weighty enough to make up for any lack of size. In fact, the smaller they are the more substantial."

At any rate, the series momentum had swung toward the Americans, who now only needed to win one of two games at the Huntington Street Grounds in order to wrap things up and become the first official baseball World Champion of the twentieth century. The first seven games had aroused deep passions, not only in the competing cities but across the country. It was clear that the idea of an annual meeting between the champions of the two major leagues was a worthy idea.

"It has surprised me to see the amount of interest that is being taken in this series," said Capt. Collins. "I never thought that it would arouse so much enthusiasm. I am glad Pittsburg won the National League pennant, for this series with the Pirates has been the most exciting of any in which I have participated. It will certainly be a high honor if we can succeed in winning the world's championship from such a bunch of sterling ballplayers as Fred Clarke has here."

Collins took the occasion to re-affirm his admiration for the great Cy Young. "I felt confident Cy would do the trick and that we would bat Phillippe enough to win. Cy pitched grandly."

We were, of course, still waiting for even one person on the Boston side to acknowledge the obvious pitching handicap under which the Pittsburg side was operating. Or did the Americans think it was normal to see one man start against them four times in seven games spread over 10 days?

Fred Clarke, Gentleman of the Plains, would let others make the appropriate excuses. "I am much disappointed," he said. "I felt all confidence we would win today, and that meant, in my opinion, the series. I have not given up yet. Look out for Monday."

The Royal Rooters came away from the game feeling the Series would not last more than one game back on home turf. They cheered and so mobbed the ball club after winning Game 7 that it took the team 15 minutes to break through them and return to the hotel.

Capt. Collins was thoroughly impressed by the backing his team had received on the road, where 200 Royal Rooters had held their own against upwards of 17,000 Smoky City enthusiasts.

"The support given the team by the 'Royal Rooters' will never be forgotten," the skipper said. "They backed us up as only Bostonians could, and no little portion of our success is due to this selfsame band of enthusiasts. Noise—why they astonished all Pittsburg by their enthusiasm, and all Pittsburg rejoiced in the interest shown in the team by our fans."

The Rooters were becoming as famous as the players. The folks back home knew all about their Pittsburg exploits, and they were grateful. When Nuf Sed McGreevey, the acknowledged leader of the Royal Rooters, returned to his saloon, he discovered that several of his friends had decorated it in honor of his return.

The one big discovery on the trip had been "Tessie." No one had the song on his or her mind when the team and the Rooters had embarked for Pittsburg a scant five days before. Now it was the new Boston anthem.

"'Tessie' did the trick," the *Globe* quoted one of the Rooters as saying. "Ever since we began to sing that song the boys have played winning ball."

CHAPTER 18

Rather than a cartoon with a strict baseball theme, the morning paper of October 12 offered its readers an over-the-top depiction of a well-upholstered gentlemen representing the *Globe* (his cummerbund proclaiming the paper to have "The largest circulation in New England") holding out to some dancing ballplayers a box containing some medals. In the background a pirate is sitting atop a mast, all that is left of his ship, and he is yelling "Help! Help! I'm sinkin'!" The caption below the cartoon reads, "Now, Boys, Down Him again and Line up For Your Medals."

The only problem was that everyone was going to have to wait one more day. It was raining in Boston. There was no debate about postponing the game, since it was to Pittsburg's advantage. For Captain Clarke had pencilled in Sam Leever as his starting pitcher, and poor Sam could barely raise his right arm.

Capt. Clarke was continuing to put up his brave front. "Talk about the Boston's receiving medals from General Taylor," he said. "I know this offer was very sportsmanlike, and I admire him for his enthusiasm and interest in the team, but I do not really believe the Boston players will wear these souvenirs."

The truth is that the situation was now borderline hopeless. For in addition to his severe pitching woes, the great Pittsburg leader was also getting little production from his franchise player at shortstop. Wagner had not been very Wagnerian, either at the plate or in the field, and had actually been outplayed by Boston's diminutive shortstop, Freddy Parent.

Wagner wasn't feeling good. His arm was giving him trouble, and his arm was his personal pride and joy. He was so publicly despondent that he talked about quitting the game for good. One devilish Boston patron saw that quote and immediately dispatched a copy of morticians' trade journal entitled "American Undertaker" to Wagner, who, by all accounts, was not amused.

Back home in the Smoky City, some people still could not get over the idea that Boston just might be better, especially considering the Pirates' well-publicized pitching woes. So it was that a rumor was being floated that the reason for Pittsburg's 3-4 situation was because the fix had to be in. The Pirates were extending the series to the full 9 games in order to make more money from the gate receipts.

The teams spent a leisurely day off. Many players on both teams attended the evening performance of "The Billionaire" at the Colonial Theatre. The house band did not forget to play "Tessie."

The day of rain led to one obvious lineup change. Clarke was able to scratch Leever as the starter and replace him with—who else?—Phillippe.

Capt. Collins was ready with Big Bill Dinneen, who, when last seen, was in full command of the situation "in the box," and who would be working with a whopping and, by the standards of the day, a shamefully exorbitant four days rest.

Tim Murnane had on his Boston hat as he sat down to the typewriter. "Billy Dinneen was in grand form against Pittsburg," he wrote, "and will throw his best curves today, and try hard to give the visitors a chance to catch a late train for home, thereby saving them one day's expense."

Murnane concluded his dispatch by saying, "The game should be a good one to watch. Take along your rubber cushion and cheer for old Boston and the gold medals."

But everything was not so jolly among the fans. The ticket situation was not good. Something was terribly amiss. People wished to buy tickets for the grand occasion, but the club claimed there were none to be had. But there certainly seemed to be some in the hands of unscrupulous speculators, as one A.E. Miller of Malden informed the *Globe* and its readers with a letter that was printed in the morning paper.

After recounting fruitless trips to both the team's downtown offices and the Huntington Avenue Grounds the day before, and claiming that Mr. McBreen, the ticket manager, had seen a crowd of 400 people gathered and had "turned on his heel and said that Mr. McBreen was gone for the day" (and when cornered, Mr. McBreen said all the tickets had been put on sale downtown and then vanished), Mr. Miller concluded by saying, "Speculators were around there with their pockets full of tickets. It looks like a game of bunco, as I could find no tickets for sale by any one except speculators."

Plus ca change, plus c'est la meme chose, eh?

The *Globe* certainly knew that something was up. "Speculators had tickets in plenty," wrote Murnane, "and were asking $2 and $3 for them. Where they got them is a mystery to Mr. McBreen, so he said, but those who had gone to a lot of trouble to call early are willing to swear that the public was not given a fair deal.

THE ROYAL ROOTERS AT GAME 8—THE FINAL GAME—OF
THE WORLD SERIES, OCTOBER 13, 1903.

"That some one blundered badly, or stood in with the ticket specu-lators, is the honest opinion of the people who follow the game closely, and were deprived of the privilege of purchasing grand stand seats at a premium of 25 cents to a speculator.

"After the experience of the club in the ticket business during the opening series here this state of affairs should not exist. It was manag-er (Joseph) Smart's business to investigate and show the baseball public where the American club stands regarding ticket speculators."

What happened to cause this reprehensible situation has never been determined. But the fact is that on what turned out to be a glorious day for all Boston baseball followers, only 7,455 were present to see the game. It was, by far, the smallest gathering at any of the eight 1903 World Series games, and it was not because the fans had suddenly stopped loving either the Boston Americans or the game of baseball. True, the weather was threatening, but that was a secondary issue.

The repercussions were enormous. American League president Ban Johnson was so upset by the way the Americans had handled crowds throughout the series that he practically forced Henry Killilea to sell the team when the season was over.

What the crowd meant for the players was that they could actually play baseball. "The players had all the room they wished," reported the *Globe,* "although the ground rules were in force just as if there had not been a clear field beyond the bases."

It was a nice, crisp 95 minutes of baseball (doesn't it seem as if some at-bats take that long today?). The Americans broke a scoreless tie with two runs in the fourth on a two-run single by Hobe Ferris, and that would be all Big Bill Dinneen would need. He gave Pittsburg four hits, and only in the sixth did they have more than one. A double play helped him out, and from then on he was completely in charge, retiring the final seven men after walking Ritchey in the seventh, and striking out Honus Wagner to end the game. With his team providing him an insurance run in the sixth (LaChance triple, Ferris single), Big Bill Dinneen pitched the Boston Americans to the first twentieth century World's Championship, 3-0.

"There was no anticlimax in the game of yesterday," reported Murnane. "A theatrical manager could hardly have worked the incidents better as to gradually warm up the crowd. The game opened nicely, evenly and smoothly, with a chance to yell every once in a while. But not until the fourth inning, not until the crowd had become thoroughly imbued with the intensity which appeared in the features of every player, was the opportunity for a grand, tumultuous outburst."

The fourth inning was superb theatre. The gritty Phillippe, making his fifth start of the series, had managed to blank the Americans for three innings and the natives were getting fretful. But Freeman opened with a triple over the ropes in center to the accompaniment of "Tessie." Parent was safe when catcher Phelps bobbed his dribbler, Freeman holding at third. LaChance grounded out, first baseman to pitcher covering, moving Parent to second as Freeman, in the fashion of countless Red Sox sluggers to come, cautiously remained anchored at third.

That brought up Hobe Ferris, who singled sharply to right-center, bringing home Freeman and Parent, at which time, according to Tim Murnane, (clearly as pumped up as he'd ever been while covering a baseball game), "the rooters tipped over their chairs in their eagerness to rise to the occasion."

Continuing on, Murnane reported that "It seemed as if every man on both bleachers was on his feet, waving his hat and roaring. A party of six at the end of the first base bleachers released large American flags to the breeze. More 'Tessie' with the band accompanying, and more shouting took place."

After the third run came across in the sixth, Murnane said the fans "anxiously watched Dinneen hurl the ball with a speed he had not attempted at any previous part in the game."

Reaching the ninth, he dispatched Clarke and Leach on fly balls. That brought up Wagner, who was experiencing a miserable (6-for-26, one extra-base hit) series. Big Bill reacted as if he were protecting a one-run lead with the bases loaded in the ninth.

Again, from the fertile brain of Mr. Tim Murnane:

"How Dinneen did rip that black ball over the plate! Three times did Wagner try to connect, but not a sound from the rooters until the last swing, which nearly carried him off his feet, proclaimed the downfall of the mighty men and his nine."

Dinneen's own take was a bit tamer: "I threw him a fast ball, and he took a cut and missed for the third strike which ended the series."

The Boston Americans were champions of the known baseball world.

Lou Criger hurled the baseball in the air, and the crowd stampede was on. As the band cranked out yet another "Tessie," thousands swarmed on the field as Captain Fred Clarke attempted to extend his congratulations to both his counterpart Jimmy Collins and the Boston players. But soon the fans had every player in the air but Ferris, who somehow eluded them. Collins was placed at particular risk. "Jimmy

THE GREAT HONUS WAGNER, ONE OF THE TOP 10 HITTERS OF ALL
TIME, STRUCK OUT TO END THE FIRST WORLD SERIES.

Collins was nearly dismembered," reported Murnane, "because the crowd that had his right leg insisted on going in a different direction than the party which held possession of his left one. Sympathetic grandstand shouters had to admonish his captors to let him down."

According to *Reach's Official American League Guide*, "the world's champions were borne to their dressing rooms on the shoulders of thousands and the cheering lasted many minutes."

Before leaving the field, the band struck up "The Star Spangled Banner," after which time the patrons left the field and continued to celebrate on their way home.

Everyone seemed to be in agreement that the teams had done honor to the game of baseball.

"This shows that baseball is the greatest outdoor sport that has ever been known," Murnane proclaimed, "and is thoroughly American, combining everything in the way of athletic skill, nerve, grit and honesty, and all that is best in our national character."

From the *Pittsburg Dispatch* came the following: "The series of ball games for the world's championship honors came to a close in Boston yesterday, when the team representing that city signalized its fourth consecutive victory over the National champions by a shutout in a contest marked by much brilliant playing. . . .

"While such a result was unlooked for by the loyal followers of the home team, and while their disappointment is consequently keen, the truth must be acknowledged that the National leaders were fairly and squarely outplayed. A test of ability involving eight games was sufficiently ample to give both organizations all necessary opportunity to show their best, and no unfair advantages were taken on either side from start to finish. In nearly all essential features of high-class play the Boston's showed themselves the superiors of their opponents during the series and their success was merited."

Collins went into the locker room, sat down and attempted to collect his thoughts. It had been a long and stressful season, and the great player-manager was physically and mentally exhausted. Then the door swung open and in walked Senator M.J. Sullivan, followed by a few of Collins' friends. Mr. Sullivan walked over to Collins, produced a box and motioned for the players to join him.

"I have been selected to present you with a slight token of esteem from the players whom you have so successfully led to victory this year," Sullivan intoned. He then presented Collins with an open-face gold watch, to which was attached an attractive fob, and suspended from that was a gold locket, in the center of which was a large diamond.

The inscription read "To James J. Collins. From the players of the Boston baseball club, American league, Oct. 15, 1903."

"I thank you," said Collins. "I cannot express what this means to me. Boys, I wish you all a splendid winter."

Collins took time to laud his opponents. "In Pittsburg we found a worthy opponent and a grand ball team," Collins said. "Every man on the team is a fine player and the spirit of true sportsmanship was never better exemplified than in the series just closed."

There was one other person to thank, and that would be a lass named "Tessie," who jumped on the Boston bandwagon in the fifth game and became even more important than Nuf Sed and the Royal Rooters.

Tim Murnane summed it up. "'Tessie,' an obscure maiden whom somebody loved in a ragtime melody, wasn't much in the place which the librettist and the composer built for her," he wrote. "But she has a place in history. She will go tunefully tripping down the ages as the famous mascot that helped the Boston Americans win three out of four in Pittsburg, capture the final game in Boston and with it the title—champions of the world.

"Sang by the thundering ensemble at the Huntington baseball grounds yesterday afternoon, 'Tessie' was there when anything worth doing was done. 'Tessie' was never caroled for any four-flush proposition; her chaste salutes were only for that which wins the royal wreath.

"Just as the claim of the heroine is to a high place on the first page of the history of the most famous post-season series, the words of the song have about as much to do with baseball as they did to the operation of stoking in the roundhouse across the field. But the effect is the thing; so 'Tessie' is a four-time winner."

Chapter 19

HENRY J. KILLILEA WAS A BEHIND-THE-SCENES KIND OF
GUY. HE WAS AN INSIDER'S INSIDER WHO WAS PRESENT AT
THE CREATION OF THE AMERICAN LEAGUE IN 1899; THE
KEY MEETINGS THAT BROUGHT THE AMERICAN LEAGUE INTO
EXISTENCE ACTUALLY BEING HELD AT HIS MILWAUKEE HOME.

The Milwaukee lawyer was a prominent University of Michigan grad-
uate, as anyone who ever spent any time with him would soon learn.
He loved Wolverine sports. According to his 1929 obituary, "A great
athlete in his younger days, he kept in constant touch with his alma
mater—Michigan. He was a bosom pal of Fielding Yost (the legendary
Michigan grid mentor), always staying at Yost's home on his frequent
visits to Ann Arbor. Yost, in turn, was always the guest of Killilea when
he came to Milwaukee." Killilea, we were further informed in that same
obit, "was never happier than when he was surrounded by friends talk-

ing sports. He knew them all well, boxing, baseball, football, even wrestling."

Perhaps so, but his venture into Boston baseball was all about business. He hardly spent any time in the city, and didn't even bother to attend all the World Series games. And it was at his office where the buck had to stop in assessing blame for an atrociously run World Series.

Whether or not the dignified attorney/owner ever personally collaborated with ticket speculators, the fact remains that someone in his employ obviously did. Beyond that, Mr. Killilea displayed a distinct lack of tact and common sense with regards to his dealings with both the Pittsburg team and the press, which had certainly done nothing but lavish praise on his team from the first day of spring training until the moment when Honus Wagner swung and missed at Bill Dinneen's final pitch to end the Series.

In both an historic first and last, Killilea charged the press for their admittance to the Huntington Avenue Grounds. In addition, Killilea trampled the existing protocol by making Barney Dreyfuss, as well as any other National League executive wishing to attend a game in Boston, pay for his tickets, as well.

The one nicety observed by Mr. Killilea was in regard to those much-discussed *Globe* medals. On the night of October 13, following the eighth and final game, *Globe* editor Charles Taylor received the following telegram from the owner of the Boston Americans:

MILWAUKEE, WISC. OCT. 13, 1903
GEN. CHAS. TAYLOR, EDITOR,

Am greatly pleased at action of Globe in presenting medals to the world's champions. The medals will be beautiful souvenirs for the greatest ball team in the history of game representing the world's best baseball city supported by the greatest press in America.

H.J. KILLILEA   7 P.M.

Ah, those medals. The *Globe* continued to milk the story to the end. "These Globe medals," the readers were told, "will be as beautiful in workmanship as they can be made; they will be executed with the utmost dispatch and one of them will be presented to each member of the world's championship team at the earliest practicable date, suitably inscribed. They are designed to be worn as watch charms, and it is to be hoped they may be handed down as valued heirlooms and as trophies of a famous victory."

No doubt the victorious Boston players appreciated their medals. In their day and age such gifts were highly valued. But one wonders whether the Pittsburg team might have walked away from the inaugural World Series even happier, for their owner had, as would become the phrase later in the century, put his gratitude for their efforts "in the envelope."

Barney Dreyfuss proved to be a man of his word. He did indeed give his players all of Pittsburg's proceeds, taking not a single cent for himself.

As a result the individual take for each Pittsburg player was $1,316.25 each. The winner's individual shares, meanwhile, were $1,182.00. Such a happening was yet another historic first and last.

Owner Dreyfuss was even more generous than it appeared on the surface. For his players urged him to deduct from their checks the amount of money Dreyfuss had lost on personal side bets during the Series. He declined to do so.

But the wily Pittsburg owner did throw one interesting curve ball at his boys. Each check was made out to the player's wife.

"I'm tired of this business of boys getting money and spending it," Dreyfuss declared. "There are a lot of those married men who don't know how to save money, but their wives do. I'm for the hearthstone, and if any of the boys want to get sore because I made out the checks to their wives, why, they can influence their wives to return the checks to me. I'll take the money back. There are some of this thrice-champion Pittsburg team who have no more sense of the value of money than a rabbit. They've got to learn."

As comedian George Gobel used to say, "They don't hardly make them kind no more."

The Boston players quickly scattered hither and yon, and the *Globe* was pleased to give its readers an accounting.

"Capt. Collins lives with his father, who is a police captain in Buffalo, and takes life easy.

"Fred Parent lives in Sanford, Me. He has a wife and several children, and what time he spends away from home he enjoys in rabbit hunting.

"Hobe Ferris is married and keeps home in Providence.

"LaChance is married and has several children. He lives in a little village outside of Waterbury, Conn., where he owns a nice home. George takes things easy during the off season.

"Lou Criger and George Cuppy run a bowling alley at Elkhart, Ind.

"Jake Stahl will study law this winter in Chicago.

"Charley Farrell takes it easy, dividing his time between Boston and Marlboro.

"Cy Young and Mrs. Young return to their country home just outside of Cleveland.

"Billy Dinneen spends the winter at his home in Syracuse and has no business cares. He is very fond of the theatre. Dinneen has some money invested with his brother in oil wells.

"George Winters will teach a district school at New Providence, Penn.

"Norwood Gibson will take life easy at Peoria, Ill.

"Tom Hughes cuts out all kind of work during the winter and enjoys life in Chicago.

"Pat Dougherty lives at a crossroads about 20 miles from Albany. Daily visits to the post office in the grocery store take up about all of his time.

"Chick Stahl has been offered a chance to become a partner in a saloon at Fort Wayne.

"Buck Freeman goes to Wilkes Barre, Penn. to loaf until February, when he usually coaches some small college ball team."

They would all soon be receiving a nice package in the mail, according to the *Globe*.

"The gold medals offered by the Globe to the players, for winning the world's championship," the readers were informed, "are being made and in a few days will be forwarded to the boys."

The 1903 season was now officially over. The Boston Americans were formally established as the best baseball team in a land that truly cherished the sport.

Oct 13th 1903

Boston and Pittsburg

THE BOSTON AMERICANS AND PITTSBURG PIRATES POSE TOGETHER
ON OCTOBER 13, 1903, BEFORE GAME 8 OF THE WORLD SERIES.
BOSTON WOULD WIN THE GAME 3-0, AND THE SERIES, 5-3.

EPILOG

HENRY J. KILLILEA DID NOT REMAIN AS OWNER OF THE
TEAM FOR MUCH LONGER. PRESSURED BY AMERICAN
LEAGUE PRESIDENT BAN JOHNSON, WHO WAS NOT AMUSED
BY WHAT ONE MEMBER OF THE BOSTON PRESS TERMED THE
"NIGGARDLY AND SKINFLINT METHODS" OF THE BOSTON
MANAGEMENT, THE MILWAUKEE LAWYER SOLD THE TEAM TO
GLOBE MAGNATE GENERAL CHARLES TAYLOR, HE OF THE
MEDALS FAME.

Mr. Taylor had purchased the team as a present for his, son John I. Taylor, a playboy sort. Though he angered many by some impetuous trades early in his regime (most notably an atrocious deal with New York in which Patsy Dougherty was exchanged for a no-account utility infielder named Bob Unglaub), John I. Taylor made at least three positive contributions to the franchise.

It was John I. Taylor who appropriated the nickname "Red Sox" for the team in 1907. It was John I. Taylor who secured the land and supervised the construction of Fenway Park. And it was John I. Taylor who supervised the accumulation of talent that led to the unquestioned Golden Era of Boston Baseball, the years from 1912-1918, when the Red Sox won four pennants and four World Series.

The Americans again won the American League pennant in 1904, the season highlight coming on May 5, when Cy Young became the first man in the twentieth century to retire all 27 men in a ball game. No, the phrase "Perfect Game" had not yet been coined.

But the team was denied a chance to win a second consecutive World Series because New York Giants' owner John T. Brush and team manager John McGraw refused to participate in a series against what they considered to be the inferior American League champions.

"Why should we play this upstart club, or any other American League team for any post-season championship?" thundered the ever-obstinate McGraw. McGraw learned "why" the next season, when Giants fans showed their displeasure with his decision by their decreased attendance. McGraw capitulated the following year, agreeing to (and winning) a 1905 World Series showdown with the Philadelphia Athletics.

The fortunes of the Boston team declined seriously, starting with a fourth place finish in 1905. The team actually finished last during a tumultuous 1906 season in which Capt. Collins was dismissed as manager, and by 1908 only two players were remaining from the 1903 squad, those being the wondrous "Uncle Cyrus" and his beloved batterymate, Lou Criger. At 42, the great Cy Young still had plenty left, winning 21 games, among them a then-record third career no-hitter.

(He would win 99 more games for Boston, and 122 more overall). But at the conclusion of that 1908 season Young was sent back to Cleveland and Criger was dispatched to St. Louis.

Young retired at age 44 following the 1911 season, but Criger, battling illness, actually became the last member of the 1903 Red Sox to remain active when he made one appearance for the 1912 St. Louis Brown before retiring from the game.

Without question, the most bizarre scenario attached to any member of the 1903 squad belonged to centerfielder Chick Stahl. After replacing Collins as manager for the final 40 games in 1906, he took his life by ingesting poison on March 28, 1907. He departed this life in the tiny town of West Baden, Indiana, which would later become a significant part of Boston sports lore. Forty-nine years later, in West Baden, Indiana, Virginia Bird would give birth to a baby boy she and husband Joe would name Larry Joe.

By 1912 the Red Sox were re-built, and there was a nice 1903 connection. They won the American League by a massive 14 games. Among the stars were pitcher Smoky Joe Wood (who went 34-5), and the superb outfield of Duffy Lewis in left, Tris Speaker in center and Harry Hooper in right. The manager? Why, it was Jake Stahl, the back-up catcher on the 1903 Boston Americans.

The Red Sox took care of belated business by toppling the arrogant John McGraw and his Giants in a dramatic World Series, and they would likewise defeat Philadelphia (1915), Brooklyn (1916) and Chicago (1918) in subsequent World Series to establish themselves as the baseball Team of the Decade, assuming anyone wished to proclaim one.

The great star of those final three championship teams was one

George Herman (Babe) Ruth, a left-handed pitcher of great renown who also swung a damaging bat.

For a variety of reasons, Babe Ruth was sold to the New York Yankees on January 5, 1920 (the deal was undoubtedly agreed upon days earlier but announced officially on this date). It was one of many such transactions in which Red Sox owner Harry Frazee systematically transferred the foundation of the best team in baseball from Boston to New York.

The record shows that through 1918 the Red Sox had appeared in five World Series and had won them all. They have not won any since 1918. The New York team built on the Boston foundation has won 26. Perhaps you've heard something about that.

Cy Young

HONUS WAGNER

APPENDIX

1903

BOSTON AMERICANS* ROSTER

(*They were also known as the Pilgrims, Puritans, and other nick-names. In 1907, they would be formally, exclusively, and permanently renamed the Red Sox.)

Pitchers

NICK ALTROCK

BILL DINNEEN

NORWOOD GIBSON

TOM HUGHES

GEORGE WINTER

CY YOUNG

Catchers

LOU CRIGER

CHARLEY "DUKE" FARRELL

ALECK SMITH

JAKE STAHL

Infielders

JIMMY COLLINS

ALBERT "HOBE" FERRIS

HARRY GLEASON

GEORGE "CANDY" LACHANCE

FREDDY PARENT

Outfielders

PATSY DOUGHERTY

JOHN "BUCK" FREEMAN

JACK O'BRIEN

CHICK STAHL

Reserve

GEORGE STONE

1903

PITTSBURG PIRATES ROSTER

Pitchers

ED DOHENY

CY FALKENBERG

WILLIAM F. "BRICKYARD" KENNEDY

SAM LEEVER

LEW MOREN

JACK PFIESTER

CHARLES "DEACON" PHILLIPPE

DOC SCANLAN

GUS THOMPSON

BUCKY VEIL

KAISER WILHELM

LAVE WINHAM

Catchers

FRED CARISCH

ED PHELPS

HARRY SMITH

ART WEAVER

Infielders

KITTY BRANSFIELD

OTTO KRUEGER

TOMMY LEACH

HANS LOBERT

JOE MARSHALL

CLAUDE RITCHEY

JOHN PETER "HONUS" WAGNER

Outfielders

GINGER BEAUMONT

FRED CLARKE

GENE CURTIS

ERNIE DIEHL

LOU GERTENRICH

REDDY GREY

SOLLY HOFMAN

GEORGE MERRITT

JIMMY SEBRING

1903

LEAGUE STANDINGS

American League

Team	Won	Lost
BOSTON AMERICANS	91	47
PHILADELPHIA ATHLETICS	75	60
CLEVELAND BLUES	77	63
NEW YORK HIGHLANDERS	72	62
DETROIT TIGERS	65	71
ST. LOUIS BROWNS	65	74
CHICAGO WHITE STOCKINGS	60	77
WASHINGTON NATIONALS	43	94

National League

Team	Won	Lost
PITTSBURG PIRATES	91	49
NEW YORK GIANTS	84	55
CHICAGO CUBS	82	56
CINCINNATI REDS	74	65
BROOKLYN SUPERBAS	70	66
BOSTON "BEAN-EATERS"	58	80
PHILADELPHIA PHILLIES	49	86
ST. LOUIS CARDINALS	43	94

1903

WORLD SERIES BOX SCORES

GAME 1
1903 World Series
OCTOBER 1, 1903 AT HUNTINGTON AVENUE GROUNDS, BOSTON

	1	2	3		4	5	6		7	8	9		R	H	E
Pittsburg Pirates	4	0	1		1	0	0		1	0	0		7	12	2
Boston Americans	0	0	0		0	0	0		2	0	1		3	6	4

Pitchers: WP - Phillippe   LP - Young   SAVE - none

Attendance: 16,242

GAME 2
1903 World Series
OCTOBER 2, 1903 AT HUNTINGTON AVENUE GROUNDS, BOSTON

	1	2	3		4	5	6		7	8	9		R	H	E
Pittsburg Pirates	0	0	0		0	0	0		0	0	0		0	3	2
Boston Americans	2	0	0		0	0	1		0	0	x		3	9	0

Pitchers: WP - Dinneen   LP - Leever   Save-none

Attendance: 9,415

GAME 3
1903 World Series
OCTOBER 3, 1903 AT HUNTINGTON AVENUE GROUNDS, BOSTON

	1	2	3		4	5	6		7	8	9		R	H	E
Pittsburg Pirates	0	1	2		0	0	0		0	1	0		4	7	0
Boston Americans	0	0	0		1	0	0		0	1	0		2	4	2

Pitchers: WP - Phillippe LP - Hughes SAVE - none

Attendance: 18,801

GAME 4
1903 World Series
OCTOBER 6, 1903 AT EXPOSITION PARK, PITTSBURG

	1	2	3		4	5	6		7	8	9		R	H	E
Boston Americans	0	0	0		0	1	0		0	0	3		4	9	1
Pittsburg Pirates	1	0	0		0	1	0		3	0	x		5	12	1

Pitchers: WP - Phillippe LP - Dinneen SAVE - none

Attendance: 7,600

GAME 5
1903 World Series
OCTOBER 7, 1903 AT EXPOSITION PARK, PITTSBURG

	1	2	3		4	5	6		7	8	9		R	H	E
Boston Americans	0	0	0		0	0	6		4	1	0		11	14	2
Pittsburg Pirates	0	0	0		0	0	0		0	2	0		2	6	4

Pitchers: WP - Young LP - Kennedy SAVE - none

Attendance: 12,322

GAME 6
1903 World Series
OCTOBER 8, 1903 AT EXPOSITION PARK, PITTSBURG

	1	2	3		4	5	6		7	8	9		R	H	E
Boston Americans	0	0	3		0	2	0		1	0	0		6	10	1
Pittsburg Pirates	0	0	0		0	0	0		3	0	0		3	10	3

Pitchers: WP - Dinneen LP - Leever SAVE - none

Attendance: 11,556

GAME 7
1903 World Series
OCTOBER 10, 1903 AT EXPOSITION PARK, PITTSBURG

	1	2	3		4	5	6		7	8	9		R	H	E
Boston Americans	2	0	0		2	0	2		0	1	0		7	11	4
Pittsburg Pirates	0	0	0		1	0	1		0	0	1		3	10	3

Pitchers: WP - Young LP - Phillippe SAVE - none

Attendance: 17,038

GAME 8
1903 World Series
OCTOBER 13, 1903 AT HUNTINGTON AVENUE GROUNDS, BOSTON

	1	2	3		4	5	6		7	8	9		R	H	E
Pittsburg Pirates	0	0	0		0	0	0		0	0	0		0	4	3
Boston Americans	0	0	0		2	0	1		0	0	x		3	8	0

Pitchers: WP - Dinneen LP - Phillippe SAVE - none

Attendance: 7,455

SOURCES

Benson, Michael. *Ballparks of North America.* Jefferson , N.C. and London: McFarland & Company. 1989.

Fitzgerald, Ed. *Sport Magazine's Book of Major League Baseball Clubs, the American League.* New York: Grosset & Dunlap. 1955.

Lowry, Philip J. *Green Cathedrals.* Reading, MA: Addison-Wesley. 1992.

Ritter, Lawrence S. *The Glory of Their Times.* New York: The Macmillan Company. 1966.

Walton, Ed. *This Day In Boston Red Sox History.* Briarcliff Manor, New York: Scarborough House. 1978.

The Boston Globe Library

The Baseball Hall of Fame Library, Cooperstown, N.Y.

PICTURE CREDITS